C000161647

F*CK FEAR

How to Get the Life You Truly Want

AIMEE-LEIGH SMITH

BALBOA.
PRESS
A DIVISION OF HAY HOUSE

Copyright © 2019 Aimee-Leigh Smith.

All rights reserved. No part of this book may be used or reproduced by
any means, graphic, electronic, or mechanical, including photocopying,
recording, taping or by any information storage retrieval system
without the written permission of the author except in the case
of brief quotations embodied in critical articles and reviews.

Balboa Press books may be ordered through booksellers or by contacting:

Balboa Press
A Division of Hay House
1663 Liberty Drive
Bloomington, IN 47403
www.balboapress.co.uk
1 (877) 407-4847

Because of the dynamic nature of the Internet, any web addresses or
links contained in this book may have changed since publication and
may no longer be valid. The views expressed in this work are solely those
of the author and do not necessarily reflect the views of the publisher,
and the publisher hereby disclaims any responsibility for them.

The author of this book does not dispense medical advice or prescribe the use
of any technique as a form of treatment for physical, emotional, or medical
problems without the advice of a physician, either directly or indirectly. The
intent of the author is only to offer information of a general nature to help
you in your quest for emotional and spiritual well-being. In the event you use
any of the information in this book for yourself, which is your constitutional
right, the author and the publisher assume no responsibility for your actions.

Any people depicted in stock imagery provided by Getty Images are
models, and such images are being used for illustrative purposes only.
Certain stock imagery © Getty Images.

Print information available on the last page.

ISBN: 978-1-9822-8062-8 (sc)
ISBN: 978-1-9822-8061-1 (e)

Balboa Press rev. date: 05/06/2019

Acknowledgements

Writing this book has been a lifelong dream. As someone who grew up never feeling smart enough or good enough in the classroom or around my peers, I always had to work longer and fight harder because of my dyslexia. As it wasn't picked up until later in my life, I just used to think I was 'stupid'. I know what it's like to watch everyone else through the window seemingly having an amazing time as you feel trapped inside, desperate to get outside and enjoy the fun. So, first of all, I dedicate this book to all those who have believed in themselves and their dreams enough to go outside and join the party; and to those just waking up and hearing the call to do so. It is my greatest wish for this book to inspire you and set you free.

I want to say thank you to my husband, Andrew, who saw something in me that I was blind to but secretly wished for, who inspired me to dream bigger, held my hand through the tears and stood by me through the tantrums. There were a lot of them! When I nearly gave up on myself, he never came close to that.

To my children, Dusty and Albert, who God has blessed me with: you are my greatest teachers and my true joy. Words are not enough when it comes to you two.

To my mum, who always taught me to stand tall and be proud of who I am and where I've come from.

And last, but certainly not least, to my editor Kay, who I absolutely could not have done this without because she actually turned my ramblings into a real book. Without her this book wouldn't be coming to life.

I am truly blessed. x

Contents

Foreword from the Author

'Heaven is not a place nor a condition. It is merely an
Awareness of perfect Oneness' – A Course in Miracles

Before we dive into this book, it's important I share with you some terminology I use to represent what I'm teaching so you don't get caught up with words and names and block your ability to understand what I'm trying to teach you.

As a student of a Course in Miracles, a yoga teacher and a sister to The Way of the Rose, which is a path of intuition, meditation and dedication to embodying Divine Love, I use the word God to describe an energy which surrounds us, is within us, gives us life and unifies us all. This energy is known as Prana in Yoga/Hinduism, Chi in China, Ki in Japan, and in the Native American tradition it is The Great Spirit.

To reference a Biblical term, 'It is that which God blew into the dust to produce Adam.'

This energy is also known as love, and I believe Divine love is the only truth.

Everything which exists outside of you is an illusion of fear and Ego.

Ego and fear are man-made. I use words such as God,

the Divine and Spirit to describe the energy that gives us love and miracles. These terms are ancient Universal wisdom, they don't originate from Christianity or any other man-made religion. In fact, they predate all man-made religions and help you transcend the limitations imposed by such religious organisations. I ask you to remember this so any emotional scarring or negative connection you may have with the word God doesn't influence or block your understanding of this book and how it can help you live the meaningful, purposeful life that you dream of.

I get asked a lot if I'm religious and my answer is always, 'No, but I am deeply spiritual.' It's often a struggle for some people to understand what this means, and I think this is because it means something different for so many.

This book and my work are what I call spiritual psychotherapy. Spiritual psychotherapy is a system for living in truth, connected to Divine love to achieve inner peace. I believe it's what's missing right now in most people's lives, causing a mass sense of dis-ease and suffering in our world. Too many people are living disconnected lives, stressed, miserable and meaningless, with no connection to their purpose.

The spiritual systems I cover here offer personal practices and guidance to help you wake up, take responsibility for your health and happiness, and understand there's more to your life than just existing in fear, sitting on the sidelines watching life happen for everyone else around you.

You have a purpose and a calling. The discovery of what this is can only come through connection to your True Self, which is the authentic and real you – in short, your soul – which is directly connected to God.

When you heal yourself, you heal your
children and, in turn, the world

I believe it's in living your purpose that you will contribute to a rising consciousness that is happening in the world right now, and this is how you will contribute to changing the world for the better. Through healing and transforming your own emotional scarring and oppression from a collective Ego that has been trapped in fear, you will heal yourself and, through yourself, your children and their children after them.

It's this collective Ego which keeps you asleep, disconnected from your True Self – your soul – and disconnected from Divine love, the essence of God.

The Ego keeps us surrounded by a veil of illusion. We are always kept busy, distracted and disconnected so we don't have time to wake up and take a peek behind that veil to see life for the wonderous and infinite possibilities it can and does give us.

I use the word God a lot in this book and in my day-to-day language. It took me a long time to be totally transparent about that and to use it in public because, probably like many of you, I was afraid of what people might think of me. Even though I know what I mean when I use the word God, I'm aware the name and different belief systems around it invoke strong emotions from thousands of years of misinterpretation and abuse. I hope to communicate the truth of what I feel through this book. If you have a negative connection to the word God, it's probably because you have a negative, fear-based experience with religion.

I'm asking you to let go of that fear and not hang

on to the word God if it makes you feel uncomfortable. Instead, replace it with a word or name you feel safer or more connected with, or try to open your mind and see the word God in a different light.

Some like the word 'Universe', others 'Mother Nature' or 'Spirit'. Whatever name sits comfortably with you, use it, because the energy of love is the same Divine energy of truth. It doesn't matter what you call it, because it feels the same to all of us. Let's not make the mistake of many who have come before us and let human words, projections and attachments deter us from the truth we all know and feel in our hearts.

Following the path I've laid out in this book, I went from living in fear, dreaming of fulfilling my purpose as a writer, creative and speaker of the truth, trapped in a career that was chosen for me and which I settled for because I was too afraid to face my fears, overcome my obstacles and walk my spiritual path, to someone who writes to you today to share these tools so that you can Make Time for You, 'Get Out of Your Own Way' and do the same.

This book is about facing your inner fears and learning to recognise and understand your Ego, so you no longer allow it to sabotage you. It is about the healing that comes from reconnecting to your True Self, which helps you fulfil your purpose and lets you leave a profound legacy for your children, teaching and living by example.

By fulfilling your purpose, you will live the abundant, happy life you are meant to live, changing the world in the process. I passionately believe the world is waiting for you to fulfil your purpose and share your gifts, so we can transform the world together.

I know Because I Lived It

It's insane how, as a culture, we dream our dreams yet avoid taking the steps to make them real.

Did you know your dreams are flashes of inspiration about your purpose, given to you as messages of wisdom and possibility from the Divine?

But today, having dreams and making the decision to pursue them is sometimes seen as delusional or even selfish – tragically, especially if you're also a mother. It can start young: some children are told dreams are just the fabric of their imagination, as if having an imagination is a bad thing, which of course it isn't.

Too many children in mainstream schools and society are encouraged not to dream or to use their imaginations. Instead they must concentrate on useful subjects that will help them figure out, at the age of six, what they want to do with the rest of their lives so they can contribute to the economy.

Too often, children are put into boxes and labelled as either a good student or 'needs to pay more attention'.

Any child that fits into the 'good student' box gets through the system ok but if you sit slightly outside this box and, dare I say it, dream of living 'outside the box' then you have little hope of getting through the educational system emotionally unscarred. Unless, of course, you have parents who see what I call the bigger spiritual picture.

My purpose, the reason I'm here and one of the reasons I wrote this book, is to help address the spiritually disconnected you, to reawaken the Divine feminine and reconnect you to your True Self so you can fulfil your purpose and, through doing so, bring a little more joy to the world.

I also want to teach you this way of living so you pass it on to those around you – especially if you have children, so they have happier childhoods, survive the current human emotional health crisis happening around us and ultimately change the world too, because it's our next generation who will do this. But change starts with you as the parent, the mother, aunt, or sister... the feminine whose role is to influence, guide and nurture.

As a woman you are often the cornerstone of your family and your children's health, happiness and future. However, you're also a human being, and you have gifts to give to the world. These gifts won't take you away from your children and make you a bad mother if you decide to pursue them. They'll actually enhance your capacity to be a more deeply connected, conscious mother who teaches through example how to have a fulfilling and happy life.

You know, life really does just come down to one thing, whether you're a mother or not. You have a purpose and you have gifts that are meant to be shared. These gifts were given to you to serve all beings, not just humans, but animals and the environment too. Your purpose is connected to how you uniquely share these gifts.

If you're not fulfilling this purpose and promise, it's because you're asleep and Ego is doing your living, or shall I say existing, for you.

When living in Ego you live in fear, simply existing asleep. That's not truly living. When connected to your True Self, you live connected to God and you live connected to

Divine love and in Truth; this is true happiness, and this is the key to being the best, happiest person you can be.

If you're here, reading this book, then you're ready to wake up and start living consciously, to embrace your gift and fulfil your promise. If you're already awake, then you're here to deepen your awareness and learn tools and practices to keep you on your path, and to learn how to integrate these into your life.

So, if you're happy and can connect with all that I've said so far, let's begin.

Introduction

We are in an age of crisis. Mental health issues such as anxiety and depression are on the rise in women, men and, most sadly, in our children. Stress is proven to be one of the biggest contributing factors to ill-health both mentally and physically, suppressing the immune system and contributing to heart disease, hyper tension, strokes and many other illnesses. Our current fast-paced, crazy-busy lifestyles are making us ill but why are we, as a collective, so stressed? History proves that we have seen harsher times than these, yet the level of illness is much worse today than we've ever seen before.

It is my belief that this heightened level of stress has occurred due to a deep collective disconnection from our 'True Selves' and the 'Universal, Divine' energy which connects us all. When I started writing this book, I struggled with who it was for: mothers? Business women? All women? I'm passionate about women's spiritual growth and health, so I decided I wanted it to be for *all* woman because all women can benefit from every aspect of this book in their lives. I believe there exists a huge pressure on women presently in our modern-day culture, and this pressure is contributing to a collective disconnection from our 'True sense of Self,' our feminine energy and the Divine which lives in all of us.

It's this disconnection which is leaving us too busy in our minds, living for others and not authentically living our lives for ourselves. Racing around trying to be everything to everyone. Keeping up not only with the Kardashians but with whatever lies we read or tell ourselves (I'm too tall, too small, too thin, too fat, too loud, too quiet…). This mindset, this way of life causes poor health and lifestyle choices, such as over eating, under eating, smoking, lack of exercise, or binge drinking, which further exacerbate and perpetuate the problem. We get stressed, we turn to quick-fix feel-good, not-so-good-for-us tactics which only fill the gaping hole temporarily, then we go back to living unhappy lives, we get sick and we live in a state of dis-ease.

Do you recognise any of this?

'You're not defined by the life you were born into or the parents you had or didn't have. You always have a choice'

But who am I to even write this book? Well, I was born what's called spiritually awake. This means I was born knowing there's more to life, very spiritually aware and conscious of my connection to God and the Divine. This was great in many ways: I always felt the love and support of God in my heart, I always appreciated life and wanted to do good in the world, and I always had the wisdom to know that no matter how hard life was, there was more to it. However, to say I was always a little 'different' from my peers is an understatement. I was always considered an eccentric and a little weird. To make me stand out some more I was born during the 80s in the Welsh Valleys, so, with my views on life, I stuck out like a sore thumb. As a result, I experienced a lot of bullying and had to learn early on how to stand straight and tall in being 'me'. This also helped me develop an iron-like determination and strong will to succeed in everything I do, and fuck all those who tell me I can't, which I believe is one of my best qualities.

My background was very much working class; we really didn't have a lot. At times my mother had three jobs on the go, and this took its toll on her emotional availability to us as children. My parents divorced before I can remember and I had very little contact with my father.

My childhood challenges meant I had to work hard on my confidence, my sense of self-worth and my belief in myself so I could escape the circumstances I was born into. I realised I didn't have to buy into my social conditioning or what was statistically predicted for me. Those challenges could either hold me down and stop me from living my dreams, because dreams don't come true for people like me, or I could choose to use how they moulded me into being a gobby, stubborn, often wild little girl to my advantage and fulfil my purpose in this world.

During my time growing up in the Valleys, times were hard for everyone. The closing of the mines led to a breakdown in our community and culture, which in turn led to a collective poverty mindset, which in many areas still exists today.

This resulted in alcohol and drug use being rife, not just among adults but among kids, too. There was little to no opportunity for young people. As kids we fought, we drank, took drugs, had babies when we were babies ourselves and dreamed of getting married before the age of 25. A job in the local factory was considered a good well-paid opportunity for when you left school.

Why am I telling you this? Well, because I knew there was more, I knew that my life was not determined by the circumstances I was born into. I dreamed of something else – at that point, escape mainly, and also big adventures. I always knew there was so much more to be done in the world, so much more to see, and that anything was possible.

I'm telling you this, not to feel sorry for myself but to express why I feel so passionate about writing this book and sharing my work with you. Coming from where I have, having the childhood I did, didn't set me up for a great start in life. I really should have been destined to have a baby by the age of sixteen or die of a drug overdose, but I didn't. Instead, I left the Valleys and supported myself from the age of 16. I didn't repeat the behavioural patterns of my parents, nor did I get lost in the torment of my peers. I was able to find the strength and courage, even at such a young age, to choose another path.

This strength and courage came from my spiritual connection and trust in God and the Divine. I didn't know it then, but I naturally followed universal, spiritual laws which connect us all. I couldn't name it or describe it the way I can today after many years of studying and practice, I just knew it because I felt it, and that was enough. This connection and knowing led me down a career path in mental health services, where I felt a call to help people like myself who hadn't had the best chance in life. It was a career I loved and spent 17 years in, until I left to raise my children and explore a new chapter, adventure and deeper purpose in my life.

You can't help where you come from and how your Ego has been shaped by all that surrounds you, but you can choose to see how your experiences have shaped your Ego and led to personality traits and behaviours that are either useful and positive, or not useful and possibly even work against you. With that self knowledge, you can then choose how they shape your life.

After 17 years working in the field of mental health, the most profound change I have witnessed people make in their lives, and the greatest healing I ever saw take place, has been when a practice of spirituality – through mindfulness and self-compassion-based therapies – was introduced.

It's self-awareness and faith that have had the greatest healing effect I have been privileged to witness and be a part of.

The reason I've chosen to write this book for women, and why my work is primarily aimed towards women, is because I believe we have the responsibility for, and important role in: guiding, loving and nurturing our children and future generations to ensure they reach their potential and live their best lives for the good of all beings. To reawaken the Divine feminine and restore balance to the world.

Women need to be able to express their feminine nature of intuition and emotional wisdom, healing from Divine love and the natural ability to flow with the energy of life, easily and naturally connecting with Gaia the earth. Women's true feminine nature has been oppressed, devalued and forced to live a lie as our cultures and societies placed more importance and emphasis on the perceived masculine qualities of logic, intellect, competition, ambition and the need for total control. Masculine qualities are seen as 'doing', whereas feminine qualities are of 'being'.

The result is what we see around us today. A world where we are all just doing the doing. People have forgotten they are human 'beings', not human 'doings'.

Women trying to act like men in the name of equality and feminism has given rise to some women fighting against other women through competitiveness and judgement of each other. We fight to be seen as equal to men but are often our own harshest critics.

Because masculine qualities have been revered for so long, too many of us have buried our feminine energy and instead live only from one side of ourselves – the masculine. But we need both masculine and feminine qualities to be balanced. We need the sun and the moon to find inner peace.

This imbalance of sun and moon energy, masculine and feminine, is filtering into our next generation just as it filtered into us. What's worse now is that the rise of the internet and social media means the distractions are easier and more frequent, the disconnection deeper, and our children are affected at a younger age.

To change our society and culture we need to bring more Divine loving energy and compassion back into our world, we need to restore the balance of feminine and masculine within ourselves and it's down to us, ladies, because we are the Divine Goddess in physical form. We carry her energy, and only we can ignite it within ourselves. We are the educators, the nurturers and the hope for our societies' and the world's future. What we show our children, what we teach them through our own example, is what will shape them into who they will become.

My connection to my True Self and Divine love has allowed me to live a truly blessed life. Always guided, always trusting and learning to let go and go with the flow, guided by my intuition and the wisdom of the Divine feminine within me.

Accepting the maternal call in whatever way that comes to you, if it comes to you, is a beautiful responsibility and opportunity for deep spiritual growth. It's vital to be able to hear the ancient wisdom of your Inner Teacher.

However, through love relationships, your Ego triggers are pressed like you've never experienced before. Having a child can cause a stirring of old emotional wounds which can come to the surface from your own childhood. By healing yourself now, you heal past wounds and relationships, the wounds of your own mother, and the wounds of the children yet to be born.

Our world needs you to be your best self. I don't mean 'best self' as in acquiring more material possessions or increasing your goals and working harder, or even to become busier pleasing everyone else. I mean your best, compassionate, healthiest, happiest self. Looking inwards, not outwards, and embracing and reawakening your feminine energy within you. This is how you as a woman will contribute to changing the world. The children around you whom you influence are your legacy, you owe it to them and to the world to be your best and happiest self.

I dedicate this book to every woman who has woken up and feels she has lost all sense of who she is, or who she used to be, and to those who have not yet woken up because they are a product of their environment and culture, and have never been shown how to.

I will show you how to.

Doing the Inner Work

When I use the word 'work', I see people's faces sink. They believe the work that needs to be done is about changing all those around them. But when I talk about doing 'the work' I mean the spiritual, internal work on yourself. I'm a huge believer that you can't change everyone else around you; if you want change in your life you must change yourself first. This is true for your relationships with your partner, children and everyone else.

People immediately think that work means adding more to their already expanding To Do list, but the truth is this: stress is a choice. Feeling overwhelmed, stressed and 'unable to see the wood for the trees' happens because you've mindlessly chosen to drift through life reacting to every demand for your attention that comes along.

There is another way. You can choose to be present, you can choose to do one thing at a time. It's the only way to achieve anything and get things done. You can choose to say yes or – the dirty word for most woman – NO to whatever you like. If you live your life with intention, conscious presence and conscious awareness, day-to-day and moment-to-moment, then feeling overwhelmed and stressed won't be an issue any more because you'll be focussed and clear about what you're doing, and where you're going, moment by moment and day by day.

Can you imagine starting your day, every day, feeling

clear on what needs to get done that day, certain it's achievable, and confident in how you feel about doing it, even if it relates to something as simple as the kids are back at school this week, uniforms are done, school lunches are ordered, so all I need to focus on is starting my new job! No over-whelm, no stress to get organised because you forgot to order the lunches – that's a real example from how my life used to be, by the way!

My Intention

My intention is to use this book to share a part of my journey with you. I want to share the insights I've gained and the tools I've used along the way through my career as a psychotherapist in mental health services, a devoted spiritual student of A Course in Miracles, The Way of the Rose and Buddhism – and mostly as a mother.

It breaks my heart to see women today living a life half lived and experiencing emotional and physical ill health because of it. If you're not living your truth, if you're not living from your soul and what I call the True Self then you're living a lie, and as much as you try to push this away or bury it deep inside you, it will come out. It may come out as physical symptoms of illness such as constantly getting viruses or back pain (a classic and well know symptom of emotional and spiritual disconnection manifesting in the physical body), or it may come out in mental health symptoms, such as anxiety and depression.

However it manifests, it's connected to spiritual unhappiness and disconnection, which not only affects you but all those around you, and ultimately that has a knock-on effect on the world. Think of the butterfly effect.

So it's time to do something about it because only you can. I am here to support and empower you to wake up and choose how you design and live your life. You don't have to become a world-renowned scientist or political leader, I'm not saying you are all born to become famous and have a world platform to facilitate change. Your simple happiness, believe it or not, is really important in changing the world. You are important! Your happiness is important, and it can only be achieved through living an authentic life and doing what your heart yearns for, because that's what you were put here to do by the Artist of this painting called life. And believe me when I say the Artist knows best and sees all. So have a little trust, and a little faith and anything is possible.

I've structured this book to help you learn to connect with your True Self because most of you have probably been what we call asleep since you were a child. That is, living unconsciously from Ego and just reacting to whatever comes your way, for example getting into the job you're in right now because your mum wanted you to, or a teacher told you it would be a good, safe career choice. I want you to start figuring out who you truly are, what you truly want and then how you're going to have the confidence to make it happen.

When you feel more present, grounded and connected in your relationships to your partner and/or children, you start living an inter-connected life. This releases you from feeling isolated and guilty for wanting more, which is one of the biggest reasons people hold back or give up on making their dreams or ambitions come true. For example, many women stop pursuing their dreams when they have children because they tell themselves they don't have the time now, or they feel guilty for making time for themselves. This isn't the case at all. By doing this you're not only doing yourself a disservice, you're doing your children a disservice, too. In fact, having a family is a great way to enhance your spiritual growth and motivate you to prioritise your own authentic happiness. Simply put: your happiness is their happiness.

And, by the way, you don't have to lock yourself away in an ashram or monastery and become a nun to meditate, pray and practice spirituality or self-reflection for growth – it can be done in everyday tasks. You just have to learn the basics first. Once you do, you'll find that you will gain more clarity and time as your mind becomes calmer and you begin to live with awareness. A less-speed-more-haste mindset will naturally develop in your mind. You'll also feel more energised and have deeper relationships with better communication. Once you have this insight you can never not know it – so be warned, this book will change your life.

Within This Book

Part One looks at the age of distraction we currently find ourselves in and introduces you to your Ego, fear and your True Self. I show you how you can connect with both to learn and grow into your True Self, through the practice of self-reflection, mindfulness meditation, self-compassion and prayer in a time-constrained, quick-fix society.

Part Two shows you how to fully integrate your new connection to your sense of self to deepen your relationships, especially with your partner and children. This is where you put everything you've learned into everyday practice within your relationships. Feeling more connected and spiritually and emotionally attuned to those you love will release you from self-sabotaging behaviours and beliefs such as guilt, which is a woman's biggest crippler.

At the end of each chapter I've included simple exercises and practices for you to add into your days. The idea is to give you a road map to follow to get you started on your path. You've heard the call, you're starting to wake up and see there's more here you are meant to do, now it's time to take the first steps to connecting with your True Self and true purpose.

Essential Reading

I've also included some essential oils recipes at the end of each chapter to help enhance your practice. I use essential oils every day for things such as mouth wash, focussing mine and my children's minds for work and learning, and using in my mediation to help me connect deeper with the Divine. I'm in love with them and they're very much a part of me.

However, this isn't a book about essential oils so I haven't elaborated on them too much but I have included a brief introductory bonus chapter at the back, and give a Further Reading list of some of the truly fabulous and inspirational books I have used to guide my thinking and the writing of this book.

If you do want to use essential oils as you work through this book, check out the bonus chapter first and learn a little more about them. Note: essential oils are a serious business, and require careful use so do make sure you're informed before you start using them. If in any doubt, ask advice from a qualified practitioner.

Deepen the Journey

I also suggest you get yourself a journal, if you don't already have one. Spend time when choosing it: this journal is about to become a sacred space and your best friend so really take the time to make sure you select something that speaks to you and calls for you to want to write in it.

It's a place where you can go and be completely you. Use it to complete all the exercises at the end of the chapters and to provide a place where you can reflect on your progress and observations. Remember, I've designed the lessons to flow on from each other and to be a road map into yourself, with exercises complementing each other and deepening your journey and growth as you read the book.

PART ONE

1

Fuck Fear: Life as a Woman Today

*'Consciousness is the state that induces action, though
it does not inspire it. You are free to believe what you
choose, and what you do attests to what you believe'*
– Foundation for Inner Peace, A Course in Miracles

Life for a woman today is busier than ever. But I think
it's important to examine the limiting idea that we have it
harder than women from previous generations. Yes, women
today are vulnerable to more distractions than ever, but I
would like to propose that life is not actually any harder for
this generation.

Life being harder implies that trying to run a home,
have a family and a career are what's causing the sense of
disconnection and level of stress and unhappiness we see
in our society today. I don't think this is the case. Instead,
women today fall prey to being distracted and are kept in
the mindset of being too busy because they are surrounded
by things such as unrealistic life and beauty advertising
campaigns, magazines promoting too-thin models whose

photographs are manipulated to make them appear 'perfect', social media and reality TV… the list goes on. All of these project a picture-perfect lifestyle that's unattainable because it's false, drawing women outside of themselves in a bid to find an easy, quick fix for happiness. For many it's too easy to lose themselves in the daydream of this seemingly perfect stress- and worry-free life as they try to escape the mediocre conundrum that their own lives often are on a day-to-day basis.

Watching glamorous housewives as they go about their lives, draped in jewels, fast cars and exquisite designer clothes is often a fun relief for many women, especially if their life falls closer to dirty nappies, house chores and 'what do I cook for dinner tonight?' I get it, everyone is guilty of a little escapism, and there's nothing wrong with it – in moderation and with a balanced, sensible perspective.

Unfortunately, like everything when it offers relief and escapism from internal suffering, it can become addictive and the lines between fun entertainment and a complete loss of reality often happen. The need to escape can cause addiction, which come in many forms. Addiction is not just linked to drugs or alcohol. Shopping, cosmetic surgery, watching Reality TV, or Soaps can all be highly addictive. It is often reported that Facebook is now a concerning addiction for many, with how many likes, hearts and comments you get on your latest post determining how your mood and self-esteem will be for the rest of your day!

Then and Now

To illustrate my earlier point about generational differences, let's compare women now and women in history to see if we have it harder. Take a look at a typical woman from 1917. We'll call her Sylvia. Sylvia has worked from the age of 13, when she was in service, working as a maid. She married at 17. Once married, her days were spent having babies and working in the family home. She had five children. In those days there were no modern appliances helping with laundry, vacuuming or cooking. Keeping a house and taking care of the children was more than a full-time job. When the First World War began, Sylvia also worked in the nearby munitions factory, making weapons

Before the war, Sylvia's husband's role was solely to work and make an income, and he expected his dinner on the table each evening when he came home. When he went to war, Sylvia worked, and took care of the children and household alone. There were no convenience foods or Jamie Oliver Fifteen Minute Meals, so everything had to be prepared from scratch, and bought fresh most days; no fridges.

Now let's take a look at Sylvia in 2017. Like a number of women today, Sylvia has attended university and gained a degree, with this she got a job in marketing. Sylvia works full time and her children attend school. Sylvia's husband helps with drop off and pick up, and Sylvia still does all the cooking and cleaning but is very much helped by her husband and all the modern-day conveniences. Sometimes Sylvia even has a cleaner and occasionally the family eat out.

Of course, there are many variations to both these stories,

these are simply a general summary and comparison of what women's roles were and presently are. The point I'm trying to highlight by comparing these examples is that women today do not have it harder than women a hundred years ago, we just have different problems to deal with. Women have worked in some capacity and still had children and taken care of the family since the dawn of time. It's not having a career and a family that's the problem here. To me, it seems the real problem lies in the need to reach outside of yourself for happiness, for answers and for fulfilment, keeping your mind busy, noisy and in a state of haste. I believe you must learn how to tune into yourself again to find what you're looking for. Your answers are always inside you.

Anyone can sign themselves into a monastery or ashram and meditate all day every day to seek enlightenment. But the world doesn't work like that for most of us. Your ashram or your monastery can be your relationship with yourself, or as a mother, with your children and with your partner who has embarked on this journey with you. I believe you can find time for your own self growth through the practices of self-awareness, self-compassion and meditation in amongst the chaos of daily life. You can find peace and love in a relationship with another human being with both your shadows and Egos tussling it out, both trying to co-exist and co-parent.

If you can do that and be happy, then you're well on your way to enlightenment or simply a happier, less stressed life.

What is missing today is not that women have more to do, more pressure and more stress. It's that somehow their ancestral gifts of emotional strength and wisdom, once

If you start looking outside of yourself for happiness, the void and disconnection from your True Self will just get bigger and you become unhappier. You will then feel the need to mask this unhappiness with more temporary, external pleasures, you'll judge others more and ultimately project your unhappiness on to them. Living in this toxic mindset you start to live on autopilot, never really seeing, hearing, dreaming or living. With all your desires and dreams competing with feelings of inadequacy, frustration, anger and bitterness, you lose your vital energy and become sick. Sounds depressing doesn't it… That's because for many it really is.

Because of this disconnection, some women also run from themselves when they have children. They hide behind their family life, forgetting who they are amidst the never-ending laundry, cleaning, homework and meal preparation. They mould into their family and forget about their own Divine purpose, even their own happiness, and instead of using this experience as an opportunity to grow, they use it as an opportunity to hide and stay stagnant.

This is played out in so many different ways. Some live only through their children: they're the mums you meet who can only talk about their kids or their partner. Their conversations are only one-way and can often feel competitive, with, 'My Johnny did this, that and the other.' Other mothers go into battle mode, and head in the opposite direction, spending their energy fighting and striving every day to keep control of themselves, their children, their partner and their lives. You see them fighting so hard they exhaust themselves and again end up losing who they are in the fight. Life then becomes about fighting instead of enjoying. Both reactions are equally destructive for your emotional health, well-being and ability to live a happy life setting the best example possible to your children.

You must always remember that often what you do in moderation your children will do in excess. This means whatever you do, whatever habits, thought patterns or behaviours you have, both good and bad, your children may repeat. This is why it's vitally important you understand that if you are feeling stressed, unhappy, unfulfilled and frustrated with life, wondering what it's all about, the only way for this to change is to choose to do the spiritual work on yourself. This will help you to recognise your negative thought patterns or patterns of negative, unhelpful behaviours such as laziness, gossip, low self-worth, overeating, misuse of alcohol, having an affair, arguing daily... I could go on for days.

If you can look within and be honest with yourself about these things, recognising them as responses to disconnection and fear; and if you can assure yourself that you can absolutely change for the better, then your children are not only less likely to internalise these patterns, but they are more likely to learn the skill of self-awareness, which is a lifelong tool that will set them up and ensure they have a life that is fulfilled and content.

I believe self-awareness is the greatest lesson you can teach your children. It's ok to have faults, to struggle and to experience dark times. Perfection is a myth. It's ok as long as you can accept your imperfections, your fears and your insecurities and learn from them. You can't possibly know yourself unless you can clearly see yourself.

Yet, understandably, parents don't like to hear the 'it's all because of the parents' argument. It's a huge responsibility to be a parent and – dare I say it – mothers often bear the brunt of it. Your children are your mirrors; your partner and your relationship are your spiritual teachers. Live your life consciously. In the good times, use every moment as an opportunity for growth but, even more importantly, you must also do this during the challenging times. If you can learn that, then you'll start living each day with passionate presence – where you live passionately, with purpose, and consciously allow yourself to experience each moment for exactly what it is. To live whole is to live with passion and a sense of direction and purpose. To live with presence is to live in this moment, in your body, fully embracing and experiencing life for exactly what it is. No expectation, just honesty.

It's your responsibility to be the best version of yourself that you can possibly be. If you want the best for your children, then you must expect the best from yourself: you must be their inspiration. Show them how happy and healthy you can be living your life, rather than merely existing and sleepwalking through it.

Caroline's Story

One of my clients, Caroline, married at a very young age. She and her husband were childhood sweethearts and came from the same small village where, at the tender age of eighteen, everyone seemed to want to get married. It was the done thing, so they did it. Caroline never really experienced life outside her village so had nothing to compare it to. Her hobbies were spending time with her husband and soon they

13

had two children. As her children grew Caroline committed herself to her family life and supporting her husband in building a successful business and keeping a beautiful home. However, Caroline talked of wanting more, not feeling like her cup was full. Although she loved being a mother and she loved her husband, something was missing.

With no outlet that brought her joy, she lost her connection to herself, she lost who she was. Life became stale, she lost any sense of self-esteem and her confidence shrivelled away, too. She found comfort in eating the wrong foods, and soon began to hate the way she looked and felt. She became a shell of her former self, her husband no longer recognised her, and she hated to even look in the mirror. Slowly, the marriage fell apart, and Caroline was left heart broken, and completely uncertain as to how her life would be now. She had no idea who she was, what she stood for, what she wanted, or even where she would go from here. Because of the stress of her marriage breakdown, and her heart being filled with insecurity, confusion, anger and fear, Caroline started experiencing depression and anxiety. She knew she was a mother, and a good one, but her self-esteem was so low she often couldn't see that, which reinforced her fear and anger as well as her lack of confidence. She needed to heal these to transform her life.

It was at this time Caroline and I began working together. Sometimes only when we've hit rock bottom and experienced the darkness of suffering can we actually see the light of hope and truth.

Slowly, Caroline and I worked together to rebuild her life. We started with her understanding of her sense of True Self, her mindset, developing her confidence and rebuilding her sense of self-esteem by taking time to reflect inwards and find out who she actually was without others' projections and expectations. I helped Caroline see herself clearly and what she wanted from her life, not what her husband had wanted her to be, or her parents, or even her friends.

Who am I and what do I want seem like simple questions to start with but many women, including myself for a long time, when living on autopilot, don't have the answers to these any more. The truth is, some never did in the first place, because they have never stopped to ask them. They have never taken the time to look inside themselves. Their whole lives have become about everyone else except them, as in the case of Caroline.

For me, my career, my practice of yoga and meditation alongside my spiritual journey was my way of making sure I stayed connected to what I call my True Self. In that respect I was lucky, because I had that anchor of self-awareness to keep me connected. I had a practice already established that kept me looking inwards and yet I still found it hard. At that time my spiritual practice was very much head and logic based, believe it or not. But becoming a mother led me down a path where my spiritual practice began to flow from my heart, giving it more depth, meaning and the power to transform and heal.

In Caroline's case, like so many other women I've been privileged to work with, she didn't have any of these tools and really had to start from scratch.

Becoming Aware

Self-awareness is the most fundamental key to connecting to your True Self, or staying connected during times of chaos, difficulties and busyness. You don't have to be on a spiritual path, you don't have to do yoga or meditate in a full lotus position for hours a day. You can practice self-awareness by simply keeping a journal and taking time every morning, evening (or both) to check in with yourself each day.

Journalling is a reflective practice that's close to my heart because I feel it's centring, clarifying and grounding, and it benefits me daily. When I journal it's a release and feels like I'm confiding in a good friend who's helping me sort through the chaos of my own mind. Even just ten minutes can leave me feeling refreshed, lighter and definitely more focussed and positive for my day ahead, or even to rest and sleep better at night after a tough day. This is why the first practice I'm asking you to lovingly and whole-heartedly introduce into your life and 'me time' is the practice of journalling. As I mentioned before, choose one you will like to write in, one that's a pleasure to open and pour your heart into.

Journalling is Good for You

When you journal daily, you're building a routine and changing your thought patterns. At first it'll be a pain in the arse to remember – and to do – but after a small period of time it'll feel like the norm. As with every exercise and practice here it's going to feel like you're learning something new, and when learning something new you can often feel overwhelmed if you have the mindset of 'it's just another thing for me to do'. But if you shift your intention slightly and cultivate a feeling of gratitude for the space to reflect and make time for yourself, I guarantee you'll stick to the exercises and practices, and before you know it you'll be reaping the benefits, which will make you want to do them even more.

Those people you see who seem to be kicking arse and making all their dreams come true, the ones you watch from afar and wonder how the hell they do it, well here's a secret: they don't have more intelligence than you, they haven't even necessarily had better opportunities than you. So what's their secret? It's their mindset, and the determination to believe in and contribute to something bigger, whatever that may be. They have practices and rituals that they do every day to focus and set their intentions, whatever they may be.

And those who are happy, who don't just seem to be super successful but also truly happy, kind and generous, the ones who make you feel good about yourself just by being in their presence – they're the ones who understand what I share with you in this book and use it to contribute to doing good in the world and making a positive impact. Their purpose and meaning in life is about others, not themselves. They get up every day and do the inner work so they can be of service, and they're grateful for it. They don't view it as another chore to do, they view it as an opportunity to be more and to contribute more. That small shift in mindset makes a huge difference, and that's the beginning of living with Divine love in your heart.

Keeping a journal is the most basic and fundamental

'you time' process that you can engage in. If you do none of the other exercises in this book, make a commitment to yourself to do this one. It's a simple practice which will open your mind and change your life for the better.

So, let's get this new journal muscle flexing.

Journal Exercise

Start a daily journal. You should begin by spending at least ten minutes every day keeping a journal where you freely write about the thoughts, worries, dreams and goals that come into your mind.

You will need to have an open and honest conversation with yourself about where you are now in your life and where you want to go. Making time for yourself, especially if you are a mother, is crucial to staying connected with your True Self and staying grounded in the roller coaster ride of family life and parenting.

Ask yourself important questions such as:

What do I want to do right now?

What do I enjoy doing?

Where am I going?

What am I doing?

What or who is draining me or distracting me from doing what I want or from living a life that I want to live?

What did I love to do as a child? Try to remember what it was that you loved to play. This is a trigger question because it's the key to really seeing and remembering what you loved to do. As a child you hadn't yet been socially conditioned to being whatever and whoever your parents, culture, teachers – whoever – wanted you to be. Your imagination as a child was wild and free and very much still connected to the Divine and your True Self.

What were your dreams? Why didn't you pursue those dreams? When did you stop having them? For some this can be a very emotional question and can dredge up all kinds of suppressed emotions so if you find yourself getting angry or sad, tearful or anxious, try to just go with that feeling, write it down and explore where you think it's coming from.

Many adults I know never had idyllic childhoods and were often controlled, heavily projected on to or abused in some way, so they never really got to experience a carefree childhood where they were allowed to dream and play freely and openly. If this is you, then this is even more reason for you to explore your dreams and passions now. It's never too late to explore and make your dreams a reality; as an adult you have the choice and you're in control. Anything is possible.

Open Minds, Open Hearts

Write as much as you need to in your journal. Think hard about the above questions – go deep here and don't be afraid to open that can of worms. You have to dig deep and clean the puss out of a wound before it can truly heal. That's gross, but it's a great analogy and so, so true!

These are self-evaluating questions that I believe are important to ask yourself on a regular basis. They help you to keep checking in on yourself and keep an open and honest conversation going relating to your own obstacles, challenges and happiness. This is essential for growth. You don't have to be spiritual and believe in God or the Divine but, hand on heart, if you do, you'll know a deeper sense of joy and have a deeper understanding of life – in particular, your life – and you'll live with meaning, purpose and presence.

It's for this reason I ask you to keep an open mind and an open heart. When you're so disconnected from your True Self, when you feel lost, alone and have zero sense of who you are and what drives you as a person, it's very easy to get sucked into looking outside of yourself for quick-fix, temporary answers to your happiness. Alcohol, comfort eating, reality TV, shopping, social media and gossip are all distractions that keep you from tuning into yourself for the answers to your own happiness. They're temporary fillers of a deep wound and hole in your heart where Divine love should be.

Tip: try not to see journalling as another chore you have to do. If you are, consciously shift your thinking and choose to see it as an opportunity to have some time and space for yourself to talk with a close and trusted friend. Maybe see it like a relaxing hot bath when the kids have gone to bed and your partner's out.

2

Ego: See Yourself to Heal Yourself

'What you think you are is a belief to be undone'
– Foundation for Inner Peace, A Course in Miracles

Now you have started your journal to help ground you and begin the practice of reflecting inwards, it's time to elaborate a little more on understanding your Ego mind versus your True Self.

This is how I see it, from a spiritual perspective. My theory is taken from various spiritual texts including Buddhism, Yoga, A Course in Miracles and many more. However, I believe that how we all read something, see ideas and internalise these into our own belief systems and projections is different for different people. So, this understanding of the Ego mind is what comes from my heart, having connected with the above ideas and beliefs.

My personal practice and belief system is one of intuition, meditation and sharing Divine love and compassion, using all of the above to inspire and guide me.

It's important to note here that the mind is made up of

various parts which give you a sense of self and who you are. We're multifaceted, complex spiritual beings and are made up of light and shadow, persona, Ego and of course True Self. To simplify this in this book, I'm going to concentrate on the Ego mind and True Self.

The Ego mind is man-made, it's a part of your mind that has been developing since you were born. It's completely earth bound. Everything you've ever experienced around you or towards you, even your processing of your world, makes up your Ego mind. This is why the Ego mind is full of fear.

So, think about it – it begins when you're in the womb.

There's so much evidence out there now that proves the foetus in the womb experiences the world as the mother experiences it. For example, we know that cortisol crosses the placenta, so if mum is anxious, then that anxiety crosses the placenta into the foetus, and fear starts to develop.

This continues through the child birthing process and all the way into adulthood. Your Ego mind is developing, growing and most of the time is keeping you locked away from your True Self.

I believe as a baby and a child you're more connected to your True Self than as an adult because the Ego mind is still in its infancy itself. It hasn't had time to grow in strength yet to have a blindfolding hold over you. This is why children are so beautifully content with nature, and why they're so joyous: they live in the moment.

Children are spiritual beings who know and understand joy. Unless they've experienced tragedy or abusive adults, they haven't yet been tainted by the expectations and projections of the world around them. They're still connected to the Divine because they're still very much aware of and connected to their True Selves.

However, as they grow, the world around them – the expectations from parents, teachers, society – does its best to instil a sense of fear in them. This begins what makes up their Ego minds and this is what begins to dominate and direct them as they grow and make decisions about the person they want to be in the world. Any sense of the true purpose and meaning of their lives can be lost to fear.

Does this ring any bells? As in the previous chapter, think about when you were a child, what kind of child were you, what did you love to do? When did that stop, and why?

You can trace your own Ego development back through your childhood. You don't have to have had a particularly abusive childhood for this to have happened. Simply going to school and being subjected to the often-oppressive schooling environment can be enough, or your culture and community's beliefs. As I mentioned, I grew up in the South Wales Valleys during a time of the breakdown in our mining culture, which had huge repercussions on our community psyche. A way of life had been taken away, people were left feeling angry, disillusioned and fearful of the future. Generations of miners were left not knowing who they were or what they would do now and this left a deep wound for the next generation to inherit; and, boy, did we ever.

I grew up feeling like the rest of the UK didn't care about our country, that we were separate, there were no opportunities and certainly no money, no jobs and no ambition. Ambition and dreams were dirty words. Alcohol and drugs became hole fillers, and anger and resentment turned to cultural violence and suicide being the norm.

This is passed through generations as children are projected upon by the parents and other adults around them. Nobody escapes the world's projections of fear on to them. Some are fortunate to be born to cultures and people who have more of an awareness of this, more of a conscious awakening regarding this; and others sadly not.

But it's not just about abuse. Living in a materialistic culture driven by greed and temporary short-lived fixes of artificial happiness is also a huge Ego contributor. In fact, it's what drives it in the first place. It's kind of a case of what came first, the chicken or the egg: the collective Ego, also the collective sense of fear which traps us in a delusional state of mind, disconnected and distracted from the Divine and our True Selves, or the fear-based, oppressive and delusional, artificial, materialistic, consumerist culture which creates and further feeds that collective Ego mind.

Sometimes it's hard to tell where it starts and where it ends.

In my case, was the mining culture that healthy anyway? Because of it there were some really old-fashioned belief systems that were reinforced, especially around women and their place in a family and the community. Children weren't sent down the mines any more, as they once were, but there was a silent expectation that children would naturally follow in the father's footsteps. Didn't that remove choice? Wasn't that still an oppressive projection keeping people marching to another's drum beat and not their own heartbeat, their own calling?

While you're consumed in this Ego state, you're asleep. You're living an unconscious, reactive life on auto pilot. You're not living your purpose, because you're not connected

to your True Self, and it's this purpose that is the mean..
to your life. Without it you just bumble along. Knowing
your purpose, the reason why you came into this life, is
the answer to true contentment, resilience through life's
inevitable suffering, and internal, inviolable peace.

The suffering that surrounds us as a society, as a world
right now, comes from so many people being unconscious of
their sense of purpose. That ache in your heart, that feeling
of 'there has to be more' is your True Self calling you to
wake up and smell the coffee! It's time to wake, it's time to
face your Ego mind and reconnect (or connect, for some)
to your True Self. It's time to, as they say, come home. But
you're coming home to yourself and to Divine love – this
is your true home and, while you're in this place on earth
embodying Divine love, you're bringing heaven to earth.
We'll look at that further along in the book.

Walking Back to You

Take a moment now and trace your life back to your
childhood. Remember a time when you lived for simplicity,
to simply play, and see the beauty in the world, before you
started worrying about things such as weight gain, or five-
year plans. Yes, I hear you say, but that was before the
responsibility of bills and rent, or a mortgage, before having
the weight of parenting or a career on my shoulders. I hear
you, I know what you're saying, but it's not the bills that
keep you trapped from living your purpose and it's certainly
not your children or being a mother with responsibilities
that keep you distracted from your True Self and trapped in
your Ego mind. In fact, the message in this book is to help

you understand that being a mother, partner, sister or aunt, being a woman is your greatest gift and chance at healing and reconnecting (or connecting) to your True Self and the Divine – it's a spiritual strength, not a weakness.

Quite simply, what keeps you distracted and disconnected from living your dreams and getting rid of the ache in your heart for something more, what keeps you unconscious is you. It's cold and brutal to hear but it's the truth, and in your heart of hearts you know it. You must see yourself to heal yourself.

Of course, it's easier to tell yourself that the way you're feeling right now is just life, it's easy to tell yourself your dreams and aspirations are too far out of your reach because you have too much to do, or because dreams don't happen for people like you, your job is too stressful, or the best and most common one: 'I don't have time.' It's easy to make excuses, and by making excuses you are choosing to remain unconscious, living in your Ego mind, living a reactive life of drama and stress and misery, living in victim mode. The spiritual path isn't easy, otherwise we'd all be enlightened right now living on clouds. We wouldn't be here slugging it out trying to make sense of it all, that's for sure.

It's not easy, but it is posible if you really want it, and oh boy is it worth it. Life is truly fun, truly magical and truly Divine, you've just got to be open hearted and I promise you will feel it too.

Fuck Fear: Don't Let the Bully Win

Your Ego mind is the bully inside you, it's the internal critical voice that drags you down when you start to rise up. It's also your self-protection mechanism, so it's not all bad. But it is limiting, and it will always strive to keep you down, locked away and disconnected from your True Self. As I mentioned, it does this because of fear. Because of all the little fears it has collected from every negative experience you've ever had since you were a child.

It does this because facing your dreams, realising your purpose is a hugely courageous thing to do. And when you do it, your Ego loses its power over you; the more you see it for what it is, the less control it has. Its grip loosens and it begins to cease to exist, and it doesn't want that.

To really start to understand the separation of your Ego mind and hear its internal voice, which is separate from the loving internal voice of your True Self, try giving your Ego mind a name. Through the journal you started in Chapter 1, begin having a conversation with your Ego mind. Make friends with it, get to know it and begin to understand all the ways in which it controls and sabotages you.

It won't just be one area of your life, there'll be many, but start with one aspect or situation where you feel its particularly powerful right now. For example, mine is writing this. I'm dyslexic and attempting to write a book! It's not a great combination. For years, despite having the dream to write this book, I couldn't get past the outlining of it. I would procrastinate and tell myself it wasn't the right time, or what a stupid idea it was anyway: you can't write a book, you can barely write a blog post, who do you think you are, you're from the Valleys and barely made it through school etc etc… it went on and on and on.

Think of something you really, really want to do, maybe go for a run to start getting fit, or lose a bit of weight, start a business, write a book, do that course you've always wanted to do that you know would lead you to your dream career. Whatever it is, take a moment, go to your journal and start to have a conversation with your Ego (if you've given it a name, use the name) and see what comes up, what are your fears, why haven't you taken action yet on doing whatever it is you want to do.

You can even keep it really simple and think of a situation you've had recently where you may have reacted to something in an angry way. Anger is essentially fear, and fear is Ego. Anything anger based comes from your Ego mind. In fact, think of every negative emotion you could experience, and they all come from fear, therefore they all come from your Ego mind. The situation you've just thought about where you had an angry reaction, is linked to a deeply buried fear within you and if you're prepared to be totally honest with yourself in the exercise above, you'll be able to see where it all leads back to – a limiting, toxic belief that you have about yourself, which is sabotaging you in all sorts of ways.

Now, you can tell me that it was his or her fault, but this is what I say to you: nobody can make you feel anything you don't already feel about yourself in some way. Nobody can make you react badly either. People can treat you badly, but your reaction to that is your choice alone, and if there wasn't already an inner demon there, a fearful insecurity buried deep inside you somewhere, you wouldn't react or respond. It would be like water off a duck's back.

Knowing your Ego, you'll understand your fears and triggers to self-sabotaging behaviours and when you know them you can consciously change them. This is true awareness of self. This is the goal of all spiritual practice. Know thyself.

And honestly this can be a dark place to go, where you need faith and you need courage, and that kind of faith and courage only comes from one place: Divine love.

Think about the situation that made you angry, and then think about how you reacted, how you managed it. Remember, you must be honest here, because self-reflection and growth don't happen if you lie to yourself. Write the situation out as you see it, describe it as if you were telling it to another. What happened, what was your response, how did it make you feel during and after? How do you feel now writing about it, is it retriggering fear for you, anger, anxiety sadness, frustration… what are you feeling?

Fuck Fear and Heal Yourself

After experiencing a childhood that was surrounded by anger and depression from the adults around me, and from struggling at school because of my dyslexia, I grew up struggling with low self-worth which manifested as explosive angry outbursts, while at the same time being a bit of a people pleaser. I was desperate to be liked, to feel loved and to fit in. However, when I didn't feel like that, I would mask the inner pain of feeling unloved and rejected, and even push people away when they offered kindness and acceptance to me. My default was always anger, I didn't know for so long how to process it, how to accept someone's love without feeling uncomfortable, like it wasn't real, so I never trusted anyone and I spent most of my life guarded and afraid.

If you had negative parents, it's highly likely you'll have limiting negative tendencies, if you struggle with low self-esteem, then look to your parents and see the connections to you.

The sins of the mother are projected on to the daughter, just as the sins of the father are visited upon the son...

As a child I dreamed of being a performing artist. I used to write my own little plays and force my brother to take part. I loved watching and re-enacting films and was never happier than when I was dancing and singing, putting on my own little imaginary productions. But they fell on deaf ears – my mum wasn't hugely maternal and had no time for dreams and fantasies. She had had an extremely tough and cold upbringing and lost her mother at the age of two. My mum never had confidence, she never believed in herself enough to dream and had no idea how to be playful. Don't get me wrong, she wanted the best for me and worked hard to make sure I was physically cared for, but she didn't have the time nor the heart for emotional nurturing and couldn't really relate emotionally to us as children. As a result, I never believed in myself enough to pursue my passions of the arts and writing. Instead, as a way to feel accepted by and worthy of my mum, I settled for a career that I never really wanted to do, which was never my dream but which was safe and respectable and which just about fit my intelligence level if I worked hard.

Because of her upbringing, my mum never believed in herself enough to become a nurse and, as a result, she lived in fear, remained unconscious and became an unconscious parent who projected her lost sense of self on to her children, sleeping her way through life with the usual short-term distractions and temporary fixes for happiness. To fulfil her lost dreams, she projected them on to me, her daughter. A career in the arts was never supported, instead it was discouraged with limiting, negative beliefs instilled into me, such as, 'You're not good enough'; 'People like us don't become actors'; 'Get your head out of the clouds', and so on. A career in nursing was pushed and I succumbed. It was safe, and actually I enjoyed it and I learned a lot from it. But it never filled the hole in my heart, the longing I've always had for more. I was never truly satisfied, no matter how much success in that field I had. I wasn't living my truth, I was living someone else's, which just reinforced my belief that I wasn't good enough to make my own dreams a reality.

Now, my telling a little of my story here isn't to feel sorry for myself or to blame my mother. She did what she thought was best, like most of us parents do. My story here is to illustrate how living unconsciously, controlled by our Ego minds, projects on to our children and the world around us. My mother's fear fed my Ego mind and became my fear, leading me to choose a life I didn't want and that wasn't aligned to my calling and purpose. This further pulled me away from my True Self and fed my Ego mind, and if you're living and parenting unconsciously then you will be doing the same to your children.

Heal yourself and you will heal the generations that come after you.

Block the Ego's Little Tricks

You can learn how to change and heal your Ego mind. First, you must understand where it comes from, and accept it as a living part of you. When you do that, and can see that what you experienced as a child (and beyond) helped create your Ego, then you can learn how to change and heal it. It's only through waking up and opening your eyes that you can see clearly. You have to know yourself and choose to set the intention to make change.

This is why understanding your Ego mind is essential to changing your life. If you stay asleep, living unconsciously from a place of fear where you experience feelings of resistance, anger, frustration, sadness, anxiety, and from these feelings engage in behaviours such as misusing alcohol, legal and illegal drugs, cigarettes, consumerism, mindless gossip, mindless watching of never-ending TV series, hedonistic behaviour, affairs, arguments, even physical aggression… the list is endless… If you do this, then you'll stay locked in the cycle of disconnection equals misery, and misery equals engaging in lifestyle choices and behaviours that keep you locked in an unconscious, disconnected state of mind.

When you live from your Ego mind you are living from a place of me, myself and I. It's blinding. Not only are you on autopilot, it becomes too easy to look outwards and blame the whole world and everyone in it for your problems. This is one of the Ego's little tricks to keep you asleep and locked in. The Ego makes it hard for you to take responsibility for your life and how you decide to live it. It encourages you to feel that everything you try fails, or the argument you just had with your husband, mother or best friend, was their fault. But, in fact, if you're brave enough to see that actually you played a huge part in the argument coming about, it will affect you less, you'll have more compassion – for yourself and others – and feel less stressed, angry, sad or fearful.

Selflessness leads to peace and contentment. If you're at war with yourself or another, or bored with the world, it is probably because you're living from a place of selfishness. Make no mistake here, the Ego is clever. Selfishness can be hidden behind the illusion of you kidding yourself that you're being selfless. It can also delude you into thinking you're the victim. This is its greatest trick, because if you feel you're the victim in a big bad world, or that you're the victim to your illness, to your circumstances, your family or even to yourself, then you lose the intention and desire to become conscious.

Drawing from my own experience with this, I can reflect on writing this book and how so many times I stopped because my Ego mind kept insisting, with every word I wrote, that because of my dyslexia and my own lack of belief in myself, it wasn't any good – nobody is going to want to read your book, you have two children and a business to run, it's not for you. You can't build your business, give up on that too; you're a terrible mother for not spending this quality time with your children; you're a terrible person for leaving a good career and financial stability therefore putting your family at risk of financial struggle… Ahhh, those conversations in my head went around and around, whirling, spinning and making me anxious and nauseous to the pit of my stomach.

So anxious, in fact, that it stopped me from writing, it stopped me trying to take the next steps in my business and, as a consequence, I became miserable at home, frustrated that I was listening to the negative voices and giving up, and resentful of my children and husband because it was their fault I couldn't live out my dream. I stayed angry at everything: myself for believing such things, the world, everything!

The tension and weight of feeling this way was exhausting. That exhaustion zapped my motivation to keep going, and that lack of motivation reinforced all the things I was believing in the first place. Can you relate to this? When looking at it through someone else's story, can you see how powerful the Ego mind is and how it can secretly sneak up on you and sabotage you from the inside out?

It would be so easy for me to blame everything and everyone else around me: my family, my dyslexia, my husband, my financial commitments, but the truth is it's the blaming, the buying into the victim mindset and the choice to let my Ego mind rule me with these thoughts in the first place that causes the cycle to repeat itself. The only way to break this cycle is to understand your Ego mind and how it sabotages you and keeps you unconscious. This understanding is achieved through self-reflection, meditation and, most of all, making the choice to see it clearly for what it is: a part of you but not all of you.

When I write from a place of being connected to my True Self, when I'm meditating, using my oils, practising yoga and am consciously connected to the Divine when I write, I write from this place of love and purpose. It's from my heart, my creative self, my soul. It flows and the words pour out of me, energising me more with every word. It's exhilarating, it gives me energy, it doesn't take it away. I could write like this until the early hours of the morning and still feel full of energy, and life the next day. Everything around me feels good because I feel content and full of purpose and joy. It's when my Ego mind decides to step in and start criticising that my joy disintegrates and the above scenario ensues.

Use the Key

The key is to understand that you're not going to be connected to your True Self permanently. The Ego mind will trigger, but the key is to build your awareness to recognise when it does, and use your tools and practices to reground yourself and return to your True Self. That's what the rest of this chapter aims to help you with. That's all you can ask of yourself and if you can do that, believe me, you'll feel healthier and happier and so will your children.

So, when you hear a little chitter chatter in your mind warning you not to do the thing you've always wanted to do 'because you can't', that's your Ego mind. When you feel your life is out of control and it's everyone else's fault, that's your Ego mind. When you find yourself judging another, that's the Ego mind. Anything negative, anything that's not connected to a loving feeling is the Ego mind. It's as simple as that.

It's not always a conscious thing, which is often what makes it so hard to recognise and accept, and it's not a bad thing either. So, don't fall into the trap now of trying to further torment yourself by beating yourself up for all the terrible judgements you've made towards others, or the self-sabotaging behaviours you may have engaged in, or for having an addiction to junk TV... oops, that might be me... This isn't about beating yourself up (more about this in

Chapter 4). Beating yourself up does not serve you and does not come from a place of love, therefore it comes from your Ego, therefore beating yourself up only serves to feed your Ego and give it more power, and so the cycle begins again.

No, to end the cycle, you not only have to recognise your Ego patterns, you have to make friends with it, forgive it and, dare I say, love it. Because your Ego is a part of you and every part of you is worth love and acceptance. Every part of you is valid and has its own beauty.

Through mindfulness meditation, self-compassion and reflection, you can make friends with your Ego, so that when it shows up, you see it clearly for what it is, a way of protecting you. It's just the part of you that is afraid – show it compassion, kindness and acceptance and your Ego will lose its power over you.

I even talk out loud to mine. When I become aware of my Ego triggering, usually through a little inner voice, I consciously say out loud, 'Thank you for showing up, I see you, I hear you, but I'm ok, I've got this. No worries.'

When the Ego mind loses its power over you, your constant need to be distracted by the outside world, because your inner world is too painful to face, lessens. The Ego voice becomes quieter and you're able to once again hear the voice of your True Self guiding you with love. Your connection to the Divine will strengthen your awareness to a spiritual sense of self, and Divine love will become more present and easily accessible. When you live in this state of mind and vibration, you'll experience less illness, less exhaustion and less emptiness.

This is where you start to feel true Divine abundance and contentment – the greatest feeling of all.

Exercise in Healing Reflection

And so now I encourage you to look at your parents and reflect on how your childhood influences from your parents are influencing you today. What has contributed to your Ego mind, what's contributing to your fears and other negative emotions or ways of being in the world? Remember, you can start to see your Ego mind clearly by being honest about your fears.

Draw a timeline over your life from childhood to now and write down all the life events, good and bad, that had the biggest effect on you. Reflect on these times and try to see the connections they have on your life today and how they influence your behaviours and lifestyle choices. This could be career, hobbies, partner, friends, eating habits, amount of TV you watch, everything! Did you have a habit?

Look at the behaviours you see (or saw) in your parents which annoy (or annoyed) you the most, then look at how you probably in some way mirror them. Jung said, that which we see in others that triggers us, or annoys us the most, has the biggest impact in terms of making us angry or frustrated – all feelings that come from the Ego. So, being Ego triggered is that part of ourselves that we don't like and try to hide.

Write down activities you did as a child which brought you joy. Are you still doing them? If not, why not? What are the thoughts that stop you from doing the things you want to do? Start writing down these thoughts and look at the way they make you feel, and then look at the reactions you have – the behaviours or things you do when you have these feelings.

Dare to be brave here, the more honest you get with yourself the better the outcome is going to be. Nobody has to see this journal, just you. Remember, lying to yourself will just keep you asleep. Sometimes, being able to receive the pain of seeing our dark side is a beauty in itself. Very few can tolerate this pain, and so they don't try to see it. But I encourage you to walk towards the fear, because you're not alone. We all have darkness in us, there's nothing to be ashamed about. We all have an Ego mind that triggers and controls and distracts us. Don't feed it with shame and fear of facing yourself.

You're just trying to build a picture of your Ego to bring it to life and make it more visible for you to recognise it when it triggers most.

In this kind of self-reflection work you don't see everything at once, things unfold as and when they need to. If you opened up all at once it would be like a can of worms exploding in your face. Your soul and your True Self know how to support you best and so usually give you a little drip feed; you never get more than you can handle and process at one time. This is a lifelong exercise and practice because there are always new situations that push our buttons and trigger our Egos. Motherhood, family and intimate relationships are your biggest button pushers! Nothing triggers you like those who know you best and whom you love, so it's vital you see yourself clearly and honestly, and then you can heal yourself and the relationships around you.

So, carry on journalling and continue on your inner journey.

Essential Oils Recipe

To go deeper when working with your Ego Mind, blend:

Frankincense: to realign yourself with the Divine.

Rose: to ignite Divine love in your heart and womb.

Ravensara: to heal old soul wounds and move forward into your future.

3

Balance is an Inside Job

*Our aim is to find balance in all aspects of our
modern day-to-day lives as individual women*

When I hear the women I work with ask me how they can change their lives to incorporate what they want to do into an already stressed and often chaotic life, my first question is to ask them why they want to do this. Is it because it's something they feel they should be doing? Or is it something they truly want to do for themselves and for the good of their family? For you to make any extra effort to get past the 'I'm too busy' and find the pockets of time in your life to incorporate whatever it is you want to incorporate into your life, it's crucial to have a very clear reason why you want to do it. You need to understand whether this comes from a desire in you from your True Self, or is it for everyone else around you, your friends, your partner, culture, society etc. It's ok if your reasoning includes the external influences, but it must also be aligned with your True Self and your desire to reach your potential and fulfil your calling and purpose.

This goes back to the understanding that if you are aligned to your True Self and living from a place of authenticity, then having children and a career, and still doing what you love won't be an exhausting chore. Don't get me wrong, it's not going to be easy either. Having a huge daily chore list of career, home and family duties won't just suddenly disappear, but when you're searching for time pockets to engage in activities that you love and that you're aligned with, then you'll feel energised, not depleted and drained.

And this is the crucial difference so I'm going to repeat it! When you are living from a place of truth, authenticity and your True Self, that thing you've always wanted to do will not be a chore and it will not drain you. Instead, it will fuel you, energise you and make you significantly happier. This will rub off on everyone around you, making them happier too, and where family and loved ones are concerned – especially with your children, if you have them – this couldn't be more true.

However, if what you're trying to squeeze into your life doesn't come from a place of truth and True Self and instead comes from your Ego and the desire to fill an insecure hole within yourself, for example wanting to keep up with appearances for the sake of not feeling bad about yourself, and fear of judgement from others, then this *will* drain you. Whatever you are doing will feel like a chore and a bore, and will stress you out and overwhelm you.

Perseverance

Writing this book took me two years. One, because of my fear- and insecurity-led procrastination; and two, because I had to fit it around a job, two small children, an often-nagging husband and learning how to build a purpose-driven business without any knowledge or prior experience. But I found the time because I wanted it from my heart, it was part of my calling and I had no peace unless I was doing something towards its creation. It didn't have to be huge amounts, I would get a sense of peace and satisfaction from just tiny little contributions here and there, but if I kept going and working on it slowly it was enough to bring about that joy and energy which fuelled me to return to the computer time and time again. This happened even when my Ego was screaming at me to quit because it felt like everything else had to get done first, or I was exhausted from a day at work, and then homework with my boys, and dinner and conversation with my husband. I was knackered, but even if I only did 20 minutes towards it before I slept, I felt good, really good. I came to realise that it didn't matter if I ever finished it, or if it ever got published because the joy and energy I got from it was enough. Once I let go of that pressure it didn't feel a chore any more, it felt like a delight and a soulful, creative, inspired activity just for me.

Does that make sense?

If you truly want to do something because your heart calls for it, it gives you the inner balance you need to feel happy and successful. Take away Ego demands and fears, such as judgements from others and pressures you put on yourself, and what you're left with is joy, not stress.

I have known athletes who hold down full-time jobs, have children and still fit their intense training schedules into their lives. And they can absolutely do this because it comes from a deep and true desire within them. It's part of their calling. So, instead of draining them, it fuels them from their soul to their mind and, of course, their bodies. This adds to their family's happiness, it doesn't take away from it. It comes from a place of purpose and passion, not a place of Ego and expectation. The difference between the two is huge: one will relieve you from pressure and stress and help you reconnect to your True Self, and therefore will leave you feeling connected, happy and living with purpose. The other will only serve to disconnect you further from your True Self and pile on the stress and pressure.

When we talk about balance today it's always in connection with the elusive work/ life balance scenario that, ironically, people spend their lives striving for. Really, what they're actually looking for is to feel grounded, content and at peace with themselves, as if their lives have meaning and purpose. This is an innate desire in us all and it doesn't go away when we have children – in fact, it gets bigger. The need to live in truth when you've had children is felt more acutely because now life isn't all about you. It's about them as well as you being the most whole version of you that you can be. That way you'll be the best teacher your children can possibly have. Your happiness is literally their happiness.

However, this longing and craving women feel when they've had children in our culture today is just chalked up to needing to do more of this and less of that. In order to feel happy, we're told we just need to find a better 'work/ life balance'.

When I hear women talk of work/life balance, I usually hear them talking about not spending enough time with their family, not feeling successful or productive at work, not being able to dedicate time to their health and wellness, never feeling fit and happy with themselves or their lives. Instead, woman I work with (and myself at one point) always talk about feeling exhausted, burned out, never seeing their kids and partners, and almost running on a hamster wheel but still not feeling they're getting anywhere – being all things to everyone, doing a thousand jobs at once but never really feeling like you're doing any of them very well.

Does that resonate with you? Because it certainly does with me. I, like many women, had this belief that somehow I would get the secret formula right between family, work and 'me time', and once I'd manged to perfect this secret formula, I'd be happy and everything else would just fall in to place. Well, I hate to tell you this, but the work/life balance you spend your time striving to create doesn't exist. It's a myth, an illusion, and trying to chase it is like a dog trying to chase its tail. In fact, I bet that's often how you feel. As if you're constantly chasing your tail.

There isn't a secret organisational formula because true balance comes from within you. It's a state of mind and a state of being in alignment. It's not about chasing anything, keeping up with others, comparing yourself, and judging yourself against society's unrealistic Ego-based expectations. Anything external to you in regard to achieving balance is just careful scheduling, prioritising and making sure that you're making time in your external world, and your day-to-day living. That stuff is just time-management skills. This is not what I'm talking about when I talk about finding your true life balance. The lay person's belief about balance, after all, is often that it's something you feel when you're productive and achieve day-to-day tasks, rather than feelings of never-ending haste and being too busy.

Just remember – you're a spiritual being in a human body having a human experience. By learning to live in the present moment with awareness of your Ego triggers, and in alignment with your True Self and the Divine, you'll find you are more productive, life will feel less hasty and you'll feel more of a sense of roundedness in your life. You'll be in alignment with your purpose and calling, and you'll see that life will start opening doors, creating opportunities, and making everything just a little easier on a day-to-day basis.

Waking up to Balance

Becoming a mother and trying to maintain my once-rigid practice of yoga and meditation helped me learn the true meaning of balance. This extended past my Ego, which was actually woven into my practice before I had children. When I was a young woman B.C. (Before Children) I had so much time to practice yoga and meditate, so much time to dedicate to my spiritual studies and growth. I was very strong, flexible and disciplined, which I was proud of and spoke openly about. I'm aware now that was probably a little boasting and judgement. We don't always see our Ego playing out so obviously under our noses, but inevitably the Divine comes along to offer up a mirror for us to see it in some form.

When my children came along, life changed in an

instant. I was knocked off my feet – literally, as I had a C-section which left emotional and physical scarring.

I obviously didn't have the same level of time to dedicate to my practice, nor did I have the energy.

And that's when I started feeling a deeper calling. I knew I could find a way to use this new life as part of my spiritual practice and weave this new journey of motherhood into it. I just needed to see if I could practice what I preached.

I also still had to deal with my Ego being triggered because of the obvious changes in my body, and it not being as flexible or strong as it used to be. The pride I had previously felt began to turn to shame and regret. I could feel myself pushing harder and becoming despondent because this persona of a yogi's body I had held on to so proudly, that I had let become my identity, had gone. That was when I started to understand yoga as a deeper spiritual practice, which was more connected to the Divine than my younger fitter self had ever appreciated.

Having a baby opened my heart to a greater depth of love than I had ever experienced before. Because of this, my True Self was able to be heard over the noise of my Ego. I began to research different yoga and meditation practices that could be developed and moulded into my new life.

When looking into my babies' eyes, when watching my children grow and blossom, I could feel all my dreams being reignited and saw life through their eyes. I saw through the eyes of a child again, which is something we lose touch with as we become socially conditioned adults, groomed to live how we or others think we should and not how our hearts yearn to live.

Everything started making sense, my whole career,

and even my perceived failed dreams, it all started coming together to make sense to me. I had always been awake spiritually, but my Ego had kept me asleep in other ways – just as it does for so many women. I was directed to teachers, books, courses – all things that were aligned to my calling and my hunger for something bigger than me. Things that led to me waking up completely, seeing the bigger picture and fulfilling my purpose.

In this kind of awakening, things only feel 'out of balance' and overwhelming if you're not answering the call and choose instead to let fear and Ego keep you asleep or distracted. I chose to wake up.

Every time I've felt driven to find a better 'work/life balance' it's been because I've been living from a place of Ego, disconnected from God and Divine love and not from a connected place of surrender, faith and trust. Inner peace has been what's lacking, because you can't find peace when you live from Ego, shut off from your True Self. If you have feelings of being unsettled, and find yourself saying things like: 'I just need to find a better work/life balance', then it's essential you prioritise making time for yourself to connect back to your True Self and to the Divine, because this is what's going to give you that sense of inner peace, clarity, courage and certainty.

Whenever I start to feel unsettled, imbalanced, and fearful of the future or I start feeling overwhelmed, it's because I've gone back on to autopilot, distracted and living in Ego. Undoubtedly, during these times I make bad decisions, which often further fuel the fire and power of my Ego, drawing me further away from connection to my True Self. That's when it is essential to prioritise making time for me to reconnect. That way, I find inner peace and clarity, and through inner peace and crystal-clear clarity, believe it or not, life is calmer, happier and more productive. It's the peace within you, created by that reconnection to your True Self, that creates the peace in your external life.

However, these moments of balance aren't given to you freely, so it's up to you to prioritise time to achieve them. I say this now before we go any further into the book to highlight the chicken and egg scenario that is prioritising time for yourself to tune inwards, grow and spiritually expand. One of the things I always hear is that women just don't have the time to take care of themselves and put their needs first. I hear this all the time: 'How could I possibly meditate?' Or, 'I'm too busy to make time for me.' Well, if you don't, you'll continue to feel you're living in haste and you'll continue to feel like you have a huge empty hole sitting in your belly, a hole that's yearning to be filled with truth, love and light.

You see the chicken and egg scenario? What comes first? Peace, calm, and living with authenticity? Good health? And then feeling good enough to make more time for yourself… but you can't have these unless you make the time in the first place. Understanding that it's only you who can prioritise the time to do the exercises in this book is what's going to help you make the shift you need. I can share my beliefs, my practices and lifestyle choices, and I can even give you some tools, but I can't make you schedule the necessary time in your day-to-day life to actually use them. Only you can make the time to let the Divine back into your heart, reconnect to your True Self and ignite the Holy Fire within.

If you compartmentalise your life and prioritise what

brings you joy, you will ultimately fuel your energy and sense of roundedness and become more productive in the long run. There's a perception that sometimes you have to be all or nothing to be successful in any area of your life where you want to excel. Whether it's being the best possible mum, wife, business owner, professional in the work place, actress… whatever is your calling and purpose. But that's all it is, a perception.

It Starts with You

I can't wave a magic wand and make you make time for yourself; it doesn't happen that way. The practices and resources in this book get used because you want to use them and you want change. Why you want change is individual to each person and that's one of the reasons why we start with the journalling process. It's also one of the reasons you need to take the time now to get super clear on WHY you want what you want. Is it your Ego? Or is it something that's aligned to your True Self? Having a clear reason why you want to do this is what will motivate you on the days where you just can't be bothered or when your Ego is bullying you and doing everything it can to deter you.

My 'why' is my children. Up until they were born I was quite happy living my life only half-heartedly, dipping my toes into the water pools of my dreams every now and again, but never throwing off my towel and diving in head first, sink or swim. I was always too afraid of failing and being judged by others.

But when my children came along I had to live harder and more fully for them. I couldn't bear the idea of them

49

having the same influences and upbringing I'd had, I wanted so much more for them. The idea of them never believing in themselves enough to chase their dreams, having a half-lived, inside-the-box life, being told who they should be and what role they should and could play in the world – that horrified me. I imagined providing them with all these wonderful opportunities of travel, and culture, inspiration and worldly insights.

Then it dawned on me slowly as I day dreamed and planned, stressing myself out working all hours to provide money for these wonderful trips, that the best example I could be to my boys was by how I was showing up in the world right now! I knew this, my training in psychotherapy told me this, I understood this theoretically like the back of my hand, but it took time for it to click with me as a mum. And like a lightning bolt it hit me, that I must embody and live the lessons I want my children to learn. And so that became my why. My dreams and goals became bigger than me, they became about being a better teacher and mother to my children, a better wife, partner and friend to my husband, and now today they're also about helping others do the same, to serve the world on a larger scale.

It breaks my heart to see women suffering, standing on the sidelines watching others' lives, comparing and judging themselves against illusions. Unhappy and yearning for the reconnection to Divine love. It breaks my heart to see the impact this has on our children and on society, the emotional and physical health issues people suffer as a result of such unhappiness and disconnection, and the impact this has on our beautiful world. With so many living unconscious, unhappy lives, they're blind to the destruction this behaviour has on us as a whole, and that we are the creators of our own misery.

So, this is now my why. As you can see from my story, my bigger why didn't happen overnight. It was a slow process of unravelling my True Self. It started with my immediate why and then moved to my bigger why and my ultimate purpose on this earth. So if you're struggling with a 'why you want what you want', then take a step back and reflect further on the questions I mentioned earlier, in the journalling exercise, and of course on those below.

Remember, when you have an emotional reason to do something you're more likely to stick to it. When your why becomes about others and giving back, it has a deeper meaning and is so much more powerful. You're a spiritual being, you're here for much more than just yourself. We're all divinely connected; your suffering is my suffering, and mine yours. Knowing and truly understanding this helps you find deeper meaning and helps you see your happiness is the world's happiness and the world's healing.

Guidance Exercise

Go to your journal now and use the following questions as guidance:

Why have you picked up this book to read?

What do you hope this book will help you achieve by the end?

What's the emotional result you hope to get from this book? Is there a financial result? (It's ok if there is.)

Is there a health-related result you're hoping for?

What purpose, cause or belief inspires you or makes you feel passionate?

What difference do you hope to make in the world, what legacy do you dream of leaving?

Whom do you want to serve? People, children, animals, the environment? Maybe all of the above?

Remember, it starts with you. You have to make time for yourself – you are a priority appointment. Whatever you need to do to do the exercises in this book, do it. And stick to them as if they were the most important appointment in your diary that your imagination can conjure up. Unless you're at death's door, you stick to them. No excuses.

Make your spiritual practice, connecting with the Divine, reflection, prayer and meditation part of your daily life. It's the best You time you can give yourself, and it's the best way to learn and understand how you can be the best version of you and fulfil your purpose and dreams.

Essential Oils Recipe

When reflecting on your Why and answering the above questions, blend:

Holy Basil: for reconnecting with the Divine.

Marigold: for vision and prophecy.

Myrtle: for summoning your muse.

4

Self Compassion: the Key to Divine Love and Achieving Your Dreams

'Love and compassion are necessities, not luxuries.
Without them humanity cannot survive' – Dali Lama

Being a woman today is a great gift for spiritual growth and as such we can offer healing to future generations and to the world. Women are gifted with the moon energies, these being wisdom, intuition and compassion.

However, one of our biggest obstacles is ourselves. We get in our own way and this is usually apparent through self-doubt and self-criticism. Every woman I know, including myself, suffers with this at times, and it can be crippling.

And I don't necessarily think it gets better with age… when I talk to the more mature of us ladies they, too, still talk about their regrets.

My biggest struggle as a woman is around feeling good enough as a mother. It seems to me that as soon as we become mothers a switch flicks inside our hearts and minds, and it's definitely related to our Ego. We feel we're never good enough for or to our children. That even making the tiniest mistake, like forgetting to pack their PE kit or forgetting to order school meals so they end up having packed lunches (hardly the end of the world), or forgetting to organise the world book day costume, is a clear sign we're terrible mothers and don't deserve these beautiful, wonderous children in our lives. I know I'm not the only one, and I know it's all a projection of my Ego, but it still doesn't stop me feeling what I feel and that is guilt!

I feel guilty if my husband's diner isn't on the table when he comes home, and I feel guilty if our home isn't clean or tidy enough. I feel guilty that I live so far away from my mum, brothers and nieces and nephews and I feel guilty because of my impact on the planet with my plastic use!

The guilt and self-judgement never ends.

And even though this can be crippling it's also the key to our greatest gift. The guilt is because as women we're deeply connected to the earth, to all beings and to the Divine. It's because we're compassionate loving beings who are here to bring balance and an awakening back to Divine love – but, if not understood, then this depth of love can feel like a burden.

This is why self-compassion is so vitally important. You may not realise it, but you emanate compassion naturally as a woman all the time. But you've been torn from your True Self and live your life externalising that compassion to all things but yourself. Giving out compassion only and not practising self-compassion to refuel and replenish your source leads to burn out and exhaustion. And what are the symptoms of exhaustion and feeling burned out? Feeling overwhelmed; anger; irritability; self-isolation both mentally (where you tell yourself you're the only one suffering and you've got it harder than anyone else) and physically; and when you shut down and lose interest in being around other people because it's just too exhausting to give any more of yourself to anyone else.

I remember when I was 17 years old catching a bus home from my little part-time job working in a nursing home. I was standing waiting for the bus when an older lady joined me. We smiled and were polite, made small talk, and then she began to tell me about her life, about her struggle with her husband and how she hated her job. I was seventeen but listened and felt a deep compassion for this lovely lady who trusted me enough with her story. She just needed someone to talk to and my face fit, or so I thought.

This went on to be a regular thing – people telling me their troubles – in fact, only yesterday I was minding my own business heading out to get some lunch when I bumped into a woman I'd only met briefly for a few moments a while back when we were introduced by mutual friends. After pleasantries were exchanged, she began telling me about her split from her husband and how she now just doesn't know what to do with herself because it's been so long since she's actually thought about what she wants, if ever she has. This is 2019 and women are still living their lives this way. Self-compassion is what's missing: the belief and intention to give yourself the same amount of kindness and compassion that you would give to a stranger, your partner, children or friends.

It's Not a Luxury, it's a Necessity

Self-compassion and kindness are being more and more researched today because they have the biggest impact in terms of ability to heal the soul, manage the Ego, and live a more positive and healthier life.

Self-compassion means to extend compassion to yourself. Compassion means to have deep empathy and kindness. When we show others compassion we're not only empathising with their pain and suffering, we are also extending a loving sense of kindness, too. So, if you put the word 'self' in front of it, this means you're offering this up to yourselves. Think about that for a moment. How often do you show yourself some compassion, kindness and love? When you're feeling tormented by those Ego bullying thoughts, and the negative core beliefs you harbour start taking over your rational thinking, or you're beating yourself up with the latest perceived failing you have as a mother, a wife, or as a woman in general, how many times have you stopped and thought, 'It's ok, this has happened because... Don't judge yourself, I forgive you, I love you.' All the kind things you would say to a friend, a loved one and even to a stranger. When was the last time you turned some of that compassion and kindness inwards?

It's not something we do in our culture. For some reason, to show yourself compassion and loving kindness is seen as a luxury or narcissistic in some way.

When I've advised clients to remember self-compassion and self-care, and take a day out for themselves to have a break and breathe for five minutes, they've literally said, 'Oh, no, I can't do that!' Or, 'What a luxury!' Or, 'I don't have time for that.' Even worse, they expressed a worry that they would be seen as self-indulgent if they made time in their lives to pursue what makes them happy, like a hobby, or if they took a nap in the afternoon because they were tired, or just felt like it.

The idea in our culture that we should give to everyone else and sacrifice our own happiness to please all those around us, not because we're serving from a spiritual place but because we're terrified of seeming self-indulgent or selfish – this idea is not healthy for us. Too often, when I suggest practising self-compassion, all I hear from my clients is, 'Oh, I don't want to seem selfish.'

I truly despair. Self-compassion is not selfish. Self-compassion is not narcissistic. Self-compassion is not a luxury, it's a necessity!

In fact, research shows that those who have an elevated understanding and sense of self-compassion are actually less narcissistic, and less selfish. They also have greater levels of self-esteem and awareness and, as a result, they have better relationships with those around them, friends, family and children.

From personal experience, working with my team and my clients, I can also see that with a solid practice of self-compassion in your life you're far less likely to procrastinate and self-sabotage.

If you look back over the chapter on understanding your Ego mind, you can see how the Ego can bully you into submission, often pushing you to give up on achieving or pursuing your dreams. Criticism from the Ego can be crippling and so painful it can often cause you to self-sabotage. Negative energy fuels the Ego. The only energy that neutralises the Ego is love. And self-compassion is essentially love towards yourself.

Compassion outwards is Divine love, the understanding that we're all connected and together in this human experience

For this reason it's clear that making room in your life to practice self-compassion would of course be a neutraliser for the negative energy of the Ego mind. This is really the only way to make friends with your Ego mind, through acceptance of it, and this acceptance comes from self-compassion. You're accepting yourself, warts and all, and loving yourself for not being perfect, whatever that means.

This is the most important practice of self-awareness, understanding your Ego and finding the strength within to pursue a life you life.

This self-love leads to a huge weight lifting off your shoulders, a release from the painful heavy burden of guilt that the Ego holds over you every moment of every day.

With this weight lifted, this fear removed, or at least understood, you feel less afraid of making mistakes and more forgiving and understanding towards yourself when you do.

Imagine if you weren't so afraid you'd fail at the something you've always wanted to do… would that make it easier for you to do it? Yes, it absolutely would!

For me, writing this book has been a real journey of facing my demons and strengthening my faith. It has taken many years to do – not because of the writing process, although that is a lengthy process to navigate, but because I had to work through so many fears and blocks of not feeling good enough to get out of my own way and just do it.

When I faced the pain of my insecurities, when I was able to show myself compassion for having the spelling ability of a 13 year old (according to my dyslexia diagnostic testing anyway), and when I was able to say to myself, 'Hey, write for the love of it, nobody has to see it, forgive yourself for not being an amazing writer and teacher like (my idols) Marianne Williamson or Gabby Bernstein…' When I was able to forgive myself, and show myself understanding and compassion in my struggle with dyslexia, and because I desperately wanted this, I was set free from the over-thinking and oppressive voice of my Ego mind, telling me that 'this is shit… Nobody is going to want to read this shit… Who are you to write this' blah, blah, blah.

It still happens. I have good days, where everything flows and I feel energised, and then I have truly challenging, painful days where my Ego thoughts are stronger and I feel my energy weaken and my focus is distracted. These thoughts, and the feelings that come with them, are heavy and exhausting.

But when that happens now, I've learned to show myself some kindness, some compassion and love, as well as an understanding and acceptance of this being my journey. For whatever reason that may not make sense now, this is who I am, this is my journey, these are the thoughts and feelings I have, and that's ok. I'm exactly where I need to be, where God wants me to be. And I even give myself a little cuddle and take it easy, knowing that once this time has passed – and it will – things will shift and energy will flow once again. And it always does.

Now imagine if, like before, I sat there beating myself up by listening to those negative Ego thoughts and feelings.

Imagine if I didn't see these thoughts for what they were, didn't understand where they came from and, instead of showing myself kindness and self-compassionate love, and giving myself a break, I just struggled on or bullied myself further. That would be adding fuel to the already pretty strong grip of the Ego. The pressure on me would increase. Eventually, the negative bullying energy would become too much pressure and I would pop, and not in a good way.

Can you think of an occasion where you've felt afraid or angry? Perhaps you can think of a situation that's happening to you now. Are you a mum trying to make your business work, or trying to bring to life your greatest creative passion in some way? Are you an artist, singer or athlete and feel you're really struggling to get everything done, serve everyone else and still give your best to your passion or business? Are you running around doing everything for everyone else, multitasking the hell out of your life but really feeling like you're failing because you never do anything the way you'd like to, or don't feel you're achieving as much as you would like to? Is this you?

Now give yourself some self-compassion. Step out of yourself for a moment and see your situation from another point of view. If this was someone else, a friend or a family member, what would you say to them?

Now say this to yourself: 'It's ok. You're doing your best. You're a wonderful woman.' Take the power away from your Ego and pause intentionally to give yourself a hug, show yourself some understanding, not judgement, not condemnation, but understanding, patience, kindness and love.

This is what self-compassion is, this is what we're so good at giving to others but seldom to ourselves.

Now feel the weight lift off your shoulders as you release yourself from unrealistic expectations, guilt and oppressive beliefs. With this light energy, you'll feel more motivated to move forward, more inspired to create, more able to sit and dedicate making time for yourself, and in turn being able to connect with your True Self and feed this beautiful cycle of self-love, creation and happiness.

This is why I believe in and passionately teach self-compassion. Essentially, this book is all about self-compassion, because without self-compassion you wouldn't make time for you; without self-compassion you wouldn't be able to fully understand and embrace your Ego mind, connect to your True Self and connect with your friends, family and society around you. It's self-compassion that will change the world, it's self-compassion that will heal dis-ease. It's self-compassion that will give you the motivation and inspiration to achieve your dreams, whatever they may be.

The Secret to a Happy Soul

Another way for us to understand and experience the importance of self-compassion is when you can understand that a lack of self-compassion leads to a feeling of isolation. Dr Kristin Neff, author of the incredible book *Self-Compassion, The Proven Power of Being Kind to Yourself*, writes that self-compassion consists of three components: kindness, mindfulness and common humanity.

Understanding a sense of common humanity helps us see that we all suffer, you're not alone in your suffering. I feel strongly that this is an important idea to understand when practising self-compassion and self-awareness as a woman living today because we have become so estranged from our inner circle of womanhood, our female family support systems. Our society – how we live in terms of family and extended family relationships – has changed considerably, especially since the beginning of the 20th Century.

We used to share our human experience together, our good times and our challenges. We took care of each other. Now it seems too often our collective Ego has generated such a fear of being women, we try to achieve everything but feel like we're achieving nothing. We're constantly plagued by images of the perfect woman who is beautiful, a kick-ass business woman and a great mother, too. How can any of us compete with those kinds of unrealistic images? And that's the word, it's *compete*.

I believe our society today, through advertising and television shows, films, magazines, pop culture – the whole lot – is designed to pit us against each other, not support each other as we once did. Because of this collective fear of not being good enough, hiding our fears and struggles from other women who are going through exactly the same pain and suffering, we isolate ourselves even further, our Ego keeps up the 'You're not good enough' nonsense, and we switch off – and stay asleep.

This is why understanding the sense of common humanity in self-compassion is vital. It helps you to wake up. When you understand that you're not alone, you don't have to feel isolated, or lonely, or as if you're the only one struggling.

We're so afraid to show our human flaws because of judgement, that nobody ever does, so we're all walking around struggling, suffering, feeling less than and beating ourselves up about it because we're so afraid to be the only one. I have witnessed this on so many levels. Only the other day someone who experiences major mood fluctuations and anxiety said to me in a fit of angry frustration and despair: 'Aimee, I practice so hard to keep myself well – I practice mindfulness every day and I have really good blocks of time where I'm feeling so good, and practising every single day, eating well and feeling really happy. But then it stops, and I start to struggle again with even being able to sit and breathe. My practice falls apart and I feel so defeated and depressed because I can't even help myself.'

This woman was so choked up with fear it was coming out as anger, anger at herself because she felt like she was the only one whose practice falls apart sometimes, the only one who sits there with a racing mind, or the only one who can't get out of bed early to practice meditation before their day starts with a manic bang. It was this sense of isolation and being the only one who couldn't 'get it right' which led to her feelings of failure and fear. The Ego mind had a hold on her and, as a result, she stopped practising and gave up because the fear, the anger and feeling of disappointment were just too heavy to bear. It was easier to give up!

I worked with her to help her see and understand that she is not the only one who experiences this struggle with her practice and her health. Even after about 15 years of studying mindfulness and personal practice I, too, still have days where I feel like it all falls apart, especially since having my children.

We all do. She is not alone, I'm not alone, and if you're reading this and have a similar experience, you are not alone.

That's not to take away from your experience; everyone's

pain and struggles are real, unique to them and valid. It's to say you're not the only one, there's nothing wrong with you specifically. Knowing this can release you from guilt, fear, anger, frustration and all the other negative, oppressive feelings we have when we feel we're the only person in the class who doesn't metaphorically 'get it' or just can't do it.

Does that make sense?

Knowing all this, can you now see that self-compassion is a necessity if you want to be the best person you're capable of being? It's essential to make time and space in your life to practice self-compassion through providing yourself with time to be you, time to pursue something in your life, time to grow on every possible level. Time to simply sit and be. This is not selfish, this is compassionate behaviour for yourself which leads to inner peace, self-acceptance and ultimately a happy soul.

Buddhists understand the importance of self-compassion. That's why they teach this first and foremost when students want to integrate mindfulness and Buddhist psychotherapy into their lives.

They prioritise the practice of self-compassion and kindness over learning about mindfulness in the sense of a disciplined practice that teaches you to focus your mind to learn how to be in the present moment.

Without self-compassion to help you cultivate a state of understanding your emotions when practising mindfulness, it's very hard – and I would say very limiting – to practice what I describe as true mindfulness.

The West has come to embrace mindfulness as a healing and beneficial psychological practice. Over the last ten to fifteen years it's become really popular. At the time of writing this book, the main buzzword in the media and pop culture is 'mindfulness', or 'be mindful', and that's fabulous. Mindfulness, as we'll discover in our next chapter, is a profoundly beneficial psychological process to heal the spirit and let spirituality grow. But only if it's taught with self-compassion leading the way. Otherwise, it's not being taught as it should be, as its true original purpose was, and so it won't be as effective; they go hand in hand.

Self-compassion leads from the heart and mindfulness the mind. They must be united for true inner peace. As I've said before, and I'll keep reiterating, you're a soul having a human experience and, as a soul, are connected to Divine love. Trying to live your life from your head will never bring true inner peace. The heart and mind must be one, you must have self-compassion and, through self-compassion, self-awareness and the desire to make a difference in the world.

There's a huge component to integrating and understanding mindfulness so that it does change your life, emotionally and spiritually, and that comes from practising self-compassion. For years I practiced mindfulness meditation and compassion towards others. But it was when I found and dedicated time to really integrate self-compassion that my whole practice deepened and grew richer. My understanding of my sense of self and my compassion for others grew deeper than I thought was possible.

Secret Ingredient

I had a toxic relationship with a girl 'friend', which at first I tried to avoid. Usually, I wouldn't have bothered with her – she wasn't my cup of tea and under ordinary circumstances I wouldn't have spent any time with her so it wouldn't have been an issue. But our husbands were friends, so I had to face the problem and, honestly, I had no idea what to do. This woman triggered me and pushed my buttons like I've never experienced. On one hand I felt sorry for her: her behaviour was often atrocious, needy, insulting, dramatic and manipulative. Or at least that's how I saw her. But she had problems with everyone, so I don't think I was the one making the drama in our situation. In fact, I was the only person who occasionally tried to make an effort with her and show a little kindness.

Anyway, it all came to a head on one occasion when I felt her behaviour was completely inappropriate and shameful and affected how I felt I was perceived by those who were around us on this particular day. So that was it. 'No more!' I said.

But it wasn't so easy – we had mutual friends and often had to be around each other. It felt a huge injustice that she was completely unaware of her poor behaviour and the trouble it had caused. Rhino skin had nothing on this girl's thick skin. She was not held accountable at all for her bad behaviour and it drove me nuts! But I knew I had to deal with it because I was the only one being affected. I couldn't rely on my usual trick of just cutting her out and not seeing her, so what could I do? I prayed, I meditated, I reflected, but nothing worked.

Then, as I was doing my usual early morning reading, I came across a passage in Lama Surya Das's book *Make Me One with Everything, Buddhist Meditations to Awaken from the Illusion of Separation*. It's about self-compassion and forgiveness of ourselves. I was reminded that most of our issues and anger towards others come from inside us. The only healing for this is self-compassion, forgiving yourself and showing yourself compassion for the issues you hold in your heart that cause you pain and cloud your vision of the world, projecting on to others.

And so I practiced Tonglen (more on this later) towards my frenemy. At first it was just a practice, but slowly it took root and spread from my mind to my heart and I didn't just think 'I forgive me, therefore I forgive you because our pain is one', I truly felt it. And as soon as that happened I was released from the burden of pain and judgement against us both. It didn't stop her behaviour. But from that point on, no bad behaviour (as seen from my point of view) or insulting ways affected me.

Don't get me wrong, we're not friends, we're still very different women, but I'm not affected or insulted by her any more. I was the one carrying the anger, and that's gone now. I know what it was and where it came from and I gave back to the light and my heart was restored with peace.

Self-compassion truly is the secret ingredient to all things happiness related.

Essential Rewiring

If you prioritise making time for you to practice self-compassion through every-day activities and also through self-compassion meditation exercises and dedicated practices, your life will grow richer. Managing the limiting core beliefs which hold you back from achieving your dreams will be easier as you'll be able to see and recognise them more clearly without the fear of the Ego bullying you into blindness because the pain is too much to bear.

Learn the art of self-compassion – and you will have to learn it, because you've been indoctrinated for years into giving to everyone else before yourself, and to believing that self-compassion is selfish, or a luxury you can't afford. All that needs to be undone; your brain needs to be rewired.

Mindfulness rewires the brain but learning self-compassion first makes this experience more powerful and beneficial than I can put into words.

Mindfulness and self-compassion sit together; one is practiced with the other. But I've put it here in Chapter 3, before the mindfulness and conscious awareness chapter, because I want you to understand self-compassion and start making room in your life to practice those exercises before you start practising mindfulness exercises. I believe this way round will make your understanding of mindfulness easier and your practice richer. Through the practice of self-compassion you'll be better able to understand the painful Ego-related beliefs that inevitably rise up when you start to pay attention to your thoughts.

Sometimes, when people begin to practice mindfulness meditation they experience a powerful surge of emotional pain from these often intrusive and painful thoughts and feelings. This is because so many people spend their time keeping busy, running from themselves and their own thoughts, that when they sit down and face them, or hear them for the first time, it can be an overwhelming and painful experience – so they don't try again.

Having a good understanding of self-compassion and an established practice will better prepare you for being able to sit with these thoughts and feelings, even to accept and surrender to them. We discuss more of this in Chapter 6: Surrender and Acceptance.

By learning how to be self-compassionate you're learning to show yourself the same kindness you would to a friend and even a stranger if you heard them beating themselves up or putting themselves down in some way.

Conscious Collaborations and Sangha

Take a moment and think about a situation where a friend has come to you where they've felt they have messed up in a big way. It can be about business, family, boyfriend, girlfriend, children – anything. Try and remember what you said to this friend to give comfort and show them kindness. What did you say to show them you weren't judging them, that actually you understood and could relate?

Knowing you're not alone in your struggle with family issues, or when building your business, helps. When it's clear you're not the only one who experiences the extreme entrepreneurial highs and devastating 'I can't go on' lows, it helps you see that it's not just you who feels that way, and you're not doing anything wrong. Knowing you're not alone liberates you from feelings of loneliness and isolation.

I started a Facebook group called 'Get Out of Your Own Way – heart-centred mindset and on-line marketing for exploding your business'. I did this simply because I was lonely working from home and, as good as my husband was, and still is, at supporting me, I needed to be surrounded by like-minded people who were going through the same challenges.

I longed for what I call conscious collaborations and

friendships, and to feel supported by those who have walked the path before me. In this way my networking company came to be what the Buddhist community call my Sangha.

Because self-love is so powerful when it comes to releasing you from the grip of the Ego, the Ego will try to persuade you that to practice self-love is to be selfish or narcissistic. In fact, as the collective Ego manifests itself so strongly in our culture, it's quite cultural now for many to believe if you practice self-love, self-care, or self-compassion you're selfish and self-indulgent. I actually have women I've worked with telling me they couldn't possibly take time for themselves to do something they love, or to relax or de-stress because it's too indulgent. This is so far from the truth. To practice self-love makes a more compassionate, loving human being. You emit this energy on to everything around you, energy of light, forgiveness, kindness. This manifests into positive loving energy around everything you come into contact with. You're giving back to the world and serving others more deeply when you can honour yourself, show yourself kindness and turn back to the love that is already inside you.

Fear has no power over love. When you love and forgive yourself for your perceived hang ups and limiting core beliefs, you can actually move past them much quicker. They'll have no power over you and this will free you from the confines of procrastination, struggle and lack of self-belief. You'll have a new sense of confidence because you'll understand at your core that there's nothing to fear. No judgement, no criticism, no sense of self-loathing, which is so exhausting and painful.

Self-love will help you let go of your resistance to change, to your success or to you mucking up and failing. Through the eyes of self-love, you see there's no concept of failing, there's only learning and growing, and there's nothing to fear in that.

Tonglen Exercise for Compassion

Tonglen is a Buddhist meditation practice I use frequently. I find it to be extremely powerful in increasing compassion for myself and others. As you've read above, it's through Tonglen practice that I first came to fully experience and appreciate the practice of self-compassion and compassion for others, so I felt it to be really important that I include it here as a self-compassion practice for you to try.

Whatever book you read, there are always slight variations on the Tonglen meditation practice; this is the one I do, and that I like best:

Get yourself into a comfortable sitting position. Make sure to sit upright and straight, but keep your shoulders and neck relaxed. You can do this in a chair or on the floor with cushions, whatever suits you best.

Now close your eyes and begin to reflect about an issue that's been bothering you recently. As this book is for expanding your mind and helping you 'get out of your own way', that issue could be about anything: your family, job, relationship, creativity, or expanding your business. For example, a concern that you're not working hard enough, or being creative enough, or being or doing enough as a mother or partner compared to the other mums you see.

Focus your attention on the thoughts in your mind right now regarding the situation which is causing you to experience suffering, sadness or even anger.

Now begin to notice how your body is feeling when thinking about this situation. Notice any tension sitting in your body, and where this tension is. Is it in your stomach, or your neck, perhaps? Maybe it's throughout your whole body?

Now visualise the upsetting thing as a dark, sooty cloud of smoke. Breathe in this dark cloud. As you breathe in, say in your mind, 'Breathing in ....' It's up to you to fill in the blank here with the negative thoughts or emotions around the challenging situation you've been thinking about. For example, if I'm feeling anxious about an upcoming speaking event, I might say to myself, 'Breathing in fear of ...' or 'Breathing in my feelings of anxiety about...'

It's okay if your breathing feels restricted at first, or you're afraid of breathing in the black sooty smoke. That's really normal and is a feeling of resistance, which is an automatic reaction to pain and suffering.

Try to relax your muscles and breathe into your belly through your diaphragm.

Many Buddhist teachers recommend imagining a window opening in your heart as Tonglen opens the heart chakra, which is the centre of compassion. When you visualise your heart chakra, see its vibrant green colour expanding through your chest.

Now, this part is really important: as you breathe out, say in your mind, 'Breathing out compassion for...' Say your name here.

Or, if you prefer, you can change the words to something else, such as, 'I breathe out...' relaxation, peace, love or freedom. I sometimes simply say, 'I choose love.'

As you breathe out, visualise the smoke now leaving your body as pure white, cleansed with love.

Tonglen Exercise for Forgiveness

Being able to forgive yourself and those around you for perceived suffering they may have caused you is vital to thriving and staying connected to your True Self. It's one of the most powerful things that Ego cannot sabotage. It's the most powerful gift we as humans have. True forgiveness of self and of others is the key to peace. It's really the final nail in the Ego's coffin.

Think of a person who's hurt you. I'm going to use the example of a mother child issue here because it may be cliché, but the mother daughter critiscism issue is very common. As you breathe in, try saying (for example), 'breathing in my mother's criticism.' Absorb it into yourself and feel it. As you breathe out, say, 'Breathing out compassion to my mother.' Keep doing this over and over until all negative feelings are neutralised.

In the example above, the criticism happened in a moment in time, and then it passed away. If you had released the initial shock and pain as soon as it happened, you wouldn't be hurting right now in this moment. Instead, you went into resistance, and the pain got trapped in your body. As you practice Tonglen, the pain resurfaces, but this time you drop your resistance and release it. Soon, the pain is gone, and you'll find compassion and forgiveness has taken it's place.

The third and final step in Tonglen is to take it to the level of the whole world. As you breathe in, say, 'Breathing in the pain of every person who has suffered like this.' As you breathe out, say, 'Breathing out compassion to everyone who suffers.' Or you can simply say, 'Breathing in suffering. Breathing out compassion.'

The reason it's important to do this is because, ultimately, we're here on earth to serve all beings and bring peace to the world by ending suffering, not contributing to it. When you practice this final Tonglen meditation you remind yourself of this truth. It's an important reminder because it's an easy truth to forget when you get caught up in your own needs. Remember again, your need isn't always what's the best thing for you or everyone else.

As you'll learn more about in Chapter 6, you won't be able to manifest properly if you're coming from a place of selfishness and thinking purely of your own needs. This compassionate meditation keeps you connected to the love and service of all beings.

Why Tonglen Works

When you first learn about Tonglen it can be a little daunting. A typical response, which includes my own, is, 'I don't want to breathe in the bad stuff, what if I get sick? How can this be good for me?'

This is the Ego's reaction. It doesn't want you to reconnect to love. And that's exactly why this practice is so powerful. It breaks open the shell of the Ego.

You've come to understand now – your Ego is in the way. When you reinforce the Ego, instead of transcending it, you get stuck. You live in fear and pain of separation, and you wonder why everything hurts – why your relationships don't work, why you fear the future, and why your achievements don't bring you lasting happiness. You are in resistance. Tonglen is an extremely strong meditation practice to loosen the Ego's grip of you.

Tip: the more uncomfortable you feel practising it, the more you need to practise it!

Sometimes you don't have the opportunity to sit cross legged and start practising Tonglen. So, although a regular practice of Tonglen is best for understanding and integrating self-compassion and compassion for others into your life to loosen and eliminate the grip of your Ego, sometimes you just need a quick reminder. When you're feeling vulnerable and exposed, try the following exercise within your self-compassion daily practice:

Think about the ways you use self-criticism and self-judgement to motivate or beat yourself up. What do you judge and criticise yourself the most for? Do you feel and tell yourself that you're too stupid or lazy, overweight etc? Try to take a moment now and get in touch with the emotional pain that your Ego voice and self-criticism cause. When you feel that emotional pain, start to give yourself compassion for feeling this way by gently reminding yourself that it's ok, you're human and you're flawed and that's ok. Think about the way you would talk to a friend who you see is suffering and criticising themselves. What would you say to them? Now say it to yourself.

Think of a kinder, more caring way to motivate yourself into taking action or making the changes you need to make to achieve whatever it is you want to achieve – what would you say? What would you do? Rest, perhaps? Again, imagine you're a wise and nurturing friend, parent, or teacher. What language would you use? Think about what you would say to gently point out how your behaviour is unproductive and even abusive, while at the same time encouraging and supporting you to do something different.

From now on, every time you hear your Ego mind criticising and judging you, first allow yourself to notice the pain of Ego's self-judgement and give yourself compassion and loving kindness.

Then try to reframe Ego's waffling by thanking it for showing up to offer its opinion, but at this present time you're ok, you've got this! This is reframing your inner dialogue so that it's more encouraging and supportive, and at the same time not getting into a fight with your Ego and adding fuel to its fire.

Remember, if you really want to motivate yourself and bypass your self-sabotaging behaviours so you can take action towards achieving your dreams, love is more powerful than fear every damn time!

Essential Oils blend for practising Tonglen meditation

When we need self-compassion, we look to the Heart Chakra. Place the following essential oils over your heart, blended with fractionated coconut oil, and/or in a diffuser:

Juniper Berry oil: the oil of facing your fears and embracing your darkness. Juniper Berry essential oil has been used for centuries within Tibetan Buddhism. It helps you hold compassion as you explore and face your Ego's darkest fears.

Rose oil: holds the highest vibration of all other essential oils on this earth. Rose is the essential oil of Divine Love. It's the most powerful healer of the heart as it opens your heart to receive Divine Grace and teaches you how to connect to this Divine Grace and love through prayer and meditation.

Geranium oil: the oil of love and trust. When trust has been lost, geranium restores trust and love through forgiveness.

Melissa oil: the oil of Light and truth. It reminds you of who you truly are, the essence of love. Melissa sparks your inner light of love and joy, to reconnect you to your True Self and God.

5

Transform and Heal
From the Inside Out

*'Your task is not to seek for Love but merely to
seek and find all the barriers within yourself
that you have built against it'* – Rumi

Mindfulness is everywhere you turn right now. The media
love it and everyone who has ever picked up a book to learn
about mindfulness has loved it so much it seems they want
to teach it!

And why not, the world needs it, doesn't it? As a society
we've never been more lost and disconnected and, as a result,
we've never been more stressed and in a state of dis-ease, and
mindfulness can and does help. In my 18 years of mental
health practice within health services, mindfulness-based
therapies had far better, longer-lasting outcomes than any
other therapy practices I experienced.

But the catch was, our rigid NHS services rely on clinics
and psychologists to get through as many service users (i.e.
patients) as they can. Because of this, those who favour CBT

(Cognitive Behavioural Therapy) use that, and only part of mindfulness is ever really taught.

What's missing is, in my opinion, the core component and key to allowing a dedicated daily mindfulness practice to really change your life through elevating your conscious awareness.

This is by far the hardest chapter for me to write because there are so many levels which make up the ideology and practice of mindfulness and mindfulness meditation, and I really want to do it justice and help you see clearly what mindfulness is and how and why it's practiced, not only from a psychological and neurological perspective, but also from a spiritual perspective – because that's where its roots are.

Yes, it's practiced widely now as a psychology and is proving to be hugely effective. There are now neurological studies which prove mindfulness can and does change the brain for the better. But, to my knowledge and from what I've experienced working within the mental health field, the spiritual component of mindfulness – its deepest and richest roots of practice – is being lost. This spiritual component is linked mainly to self-compassion, compassion for others and Divine, universal love.

As discussed in the last chapter, we still struggle as a society to embrace and value the importance of self-love and self-compassion, and love and compassion for others, which is why there remains so much dis-ease and anger tearing up our world.

The practice of mindfulness is the key to unlocking your heart and lifting the blindfold to see and experience this deep sense of universal love.

Simply put, mindfulness is being present in the moment,

with full awareness. When you practice mindfulness meditation you are setting your intention to fix your mind or focus your mind on one single point for a sustained period of time. This is known as a mindfulness meditation, which can often differ slightly from other meditations, where that intention to focus on a single point isn't always present or the objective of the practice – for example, meditations specifically designed for relaxation, where the aim is to relax and/or fall asleep. With a mindfulness meditation the intention is not to relax or fall asleep, but actually to be more present and awake. Jon Kabat-Zinn describes this as 'falling awake'. This is when you become alert and present to your full mind, body and soul experience in this exact moment.

This practice is the psychology of mindfulness, the training of your brain, and it's been proven to be extremely effective, both psychologically and neurologically.

Neuroscientists have proven that incorporating a mindfulness practice into your daily life positively affects brain areas related to perception, body awareness, pain tolerance, emotion regulation, introspection, complex thinking, and of course a sense of self or, in this case, True Self.

MRI scans show us that after an eight-week mindfulness course where you practice every day, the part of the brain which controls 'fight or flight', which is known as the amygdala, appears to shrink. This primal part of the brain, which is always associated with fear and emotions, is part of the body's response and reaction to stress and the feeling of being overwhelmed. In short, practising mindfulness every day helps you manage the fear triggered by your Ego, not just because you have psychological awareness of it, but because your brain changes in its response towards it. Boom! You can't argue with empirical evidence and neurological fact.

However, mindfulness is not just about being 'calm'. Yes, this is a fabulous bonus, or bi-product, to the understanding and practice of mindfulness, but it's so much more than that. That's not to take away from those who concentrate on teaching what I call the 'simple psychology' of mindfulness; it has its place. Not everyone is ready to go deeper and get spiritual. I get that.

For those who aren't yet ready to open their heart to the Divine, using mindfulness to stay 'calm' in a chaotic world is a good start, and I bless you all and wish you the best of health and a long life.

But for those who are ready, and who feel the pull towards something more, something greater than themselves and this very small life, keep reading because mindfulness can enrich your life and give you so much more than you think you already know and understand.

There's another side to mindfulness: the spiritual side. It's my passionate belief that unless you teach (and learn) this spiritual side, you're not doing the absolute life-changing power of mindfulness justice.

Mindfulness isn't just a new psychological intervention, it's ancient in its origins, and very much universal in the spiritual arena.

Mindfulness is a way of becoming still and present, a way of being able to hear the voice of God and connect to the Divine without the Ego and noisy world around you pulling you away and keeping you distracted and disconnected. Mindfulness is your way back to your True Self and to God.

Praying is your way to communicate, affirm and reflect. But mindfulness is the key to hearing and experiencing fully the Divine silence and nature of God. It's the key to hearing the whisper of your True Self, and your natural woman's intuition as it guides you through your life to where you need to be.

To explore this further, let's look at mindfulness and its origins, and how it sits within, yet transcends, spiritual practices which I follow, such as Buddhism, Yoga, A Course in Miracles and The Way of the Rose. I hope to show how mindfulness lies within all these systems or practices and to demonstrate how it can stand alone as a psychological practice but, when used within a spiritual practice, its meaning is so much richer and your experience and healing so much more powerful.

I've been teaching mindfulness, self-compassion and yoga as a form of therapy for many years now. Once I had two students – a husband and wife – who were prevented from attending my classes. It turns out they had been forbidden by the pastor of their Christian church to stop attending because it was felt that to practice mindfulness and yoga was in some way unholy or against their church.

It's my intention to show here that mindfulness and yoga are ways of enhancing your spiritual practice, no matter what faith you follow. If this pastor had truly understood mindfulness meditation and even yoga, they would have realised it is a way of praying to and hearing the voice and nature of God. It's a life system that brings you closer to God, through being able to step away from the fear of the Ego mind, which keeps you disconnected from God. Mindfulness does not separate you from yourself or from

God, it opens your heart and stills your mind so you can allow God to work through you for the good of all beings.

Mindfulness – Where it all Began

Let's look at the origins. We can begin by looking at Buddhism because Buddhism is a world religion, or a way of life as some, including myself, see it, and is considered to be where Mindfulness originated.

However, despite this belief, the truth is mindfulness is much bigger than that, and much older. Mindfulness sits within Buddhism, Christianity, Hinduism, Yoga and Tantra. It is ancient in its origins and transcends all man-made religions.

Mindfulness is a universal practice and experience which we can all access to connect to our True Selves and God. It's a way to quieten the mind, to be still and present, and experience the energy of the Divine and the breath of God flowing through and around us.

But, for the purpose of this discussion, here's a quick, easy-to-understand summary of how mindfulness is used within Buddhism to purify the mind, experience self-compassion and compassion for others, and help you live the eightfold path, which is really a bit like a code of conduct on how to live your best life.

Buddhist Dharma is formed by the Four Noble Truths; you are following the eightfold-path to practice and enhance your understanding of the Four Noble Truths, which are:

'I teach suffering, its origin, cessation and path. That's all I teach,' said the Buddha 2500 years ago.

The Four Noble Truths contain the essence of the

Buddha's teachings. It was these four principles that the Buddha came to understand during his meditation under the bodhi tree.

Dukkha: the Truth of suffering. This states that life can be less than ideal and frequently fails to live up to people's often too-high expectations. As humans, and because of our Ego mind, we're often subject to cravings and desires which we can't fully satisfy because any satisfaction is temporary since it's often not real and is based on external Ego desires.

Samudāya: the Truth of the origin of suffering. This comes from the root of negative desire, which comes in three root forms of 'evil', which are: a) greed; b) ignorance and delusion; and c) hatred and destructive urges.

Buddha described attachment as the root cause of suffering to both negative and positive desire. This makes sense especially in our culture today where we have this 'keeping up with the Kardashians' mentality, which I briefly mentioned earlier. If someone feels good and is 'thriving' in life, externally happy and seemingly doing well then they are happy and strive to keep this happiness. If, however, someone is struggling with moods, their relationship, job or sense of self, the common response is to hide this because of a fear of judgement, because they might feel they are a failure in society's eyes. Even to feel nothing can cause suffering, because it's typical to want to feel happy all the time, right? If we're not feeling happy then we're feeling sad – but what if you're feeling neither, just neutral? This is often confused with sad because it's not happy.

We should be learning that this state is acceptable, and that emotions – happy, sad, neutral – are all fleeting, and that it's the *clinging* to such emotions which causes the suffering, not the emotion itself. Through a mindfulness practice you can come to see and know this.

Nirodha: the Truth of the cessation of suffering. This is to know that it's fully possible to liberate yourself from attachment and reach nirvana. Nirvana is a state of being where you no longer feel the three root forms of evil as described above (greed; ignorance and delusion; hatred and destructive urges). When you experience this liberation from attachment and the suffering caused by the three root forms of evil, you become truly compassionate to all beings (including yourself). In the words of The Way of the Rose and A Course In Miracles, 'this is to know and embody love in every fibre of your being and to disseminate this to the world around you, again for the good of all beings.'

Magga: the Truth of the path to the cessation of suffering. This is the eightfold path. To follow the eightfold path is to consciously follow a spiritual practice and system of living which helps free you from the three root forms of evil of your own Ego mind, so that you embody and give love and compassion freely.

In summary, the eightfold path in Buddhism is made up of:

Right view: an accurate understanding of the nature of life, the mind, and how you see and live in the world.

Right intention: having the right intention to act honourably, and to avoid actions which come from fear, anger and attachment.

Right speech: refraining from verbal misdeeds, such as lying, divisive speech, harsh speech, and senseless speech.

Right conduct: refraining from physical misdeeds, such as killing, stealing, and sexual misconduct.

Right livelihood: avoiding trades that directly or indirectly harm others, such as selling slaves, weapons, animals for slaughter, intoxicants, or poisons.

Right effort: abandoning negative states of mind that have already arisen, preventing negative states that have yet to arise, and sustaining positive states that have already arisen.

Right mindfulness: awareness of body, feelings, thought, and phenomena (the constituents of the existing world).

Right concentration: correct concentration, single-mindedness. Focus.

It's believed if you follow this eightfold path with intention, making sure to adhere to the teachings daily, you'll find inner peace, also known as nirvana or enlightenment. This is similar to heaven in Christian terminology.

Mindfulness weaves through the eightfold path. If you think about it, without being mindful of your speech or how you see the world, you will live and speak in a reactive, unconscious way.

A practice of mindfulness connects you to self-compassion and helps you see and recognise the grip the Ego has over you in the way of fears and self-sabotaging behaviours. So if you have the right view, you see things more clearly, you hear things more clearly and you feel things more acutely and accurately.

Your thoughts determine your actions, and your speech can often reinforce thoughts and actions so having right speech is important, but you need awareness and a pause to be able to see your thoughts and monitor your speech. Mindfulness helps you do that because it allows you to pause and breathe. It helps you recognise your thoughts so you're not immersed in them, allowing them to be in control and you in a state of emotional reaction, at the mercy of them, and your emotions, speech and actions, too. Mindfulness helps you be present, grounded and in control, not reactive and out of control.

It's worth noting here that the eightfold path is also known as the 'middle way'. It avoids both indulgence and severe asceticism and looks more for balance. Neither over-indulgence nor flagellating yourself into a life of misery in the name of spiritual practice helps you achieve enlightenment.

Yoga

Let's look at the yoga system briefly and see how mindfulness fits in here.

Yoga, too, is often misunderstood by the West and is usually only seen as a form of good exercise, when in fact it has many systems and components to it which make up the whole.

Yoga can stand alone as a practice for good mind/body health, a way of reflecting, reducing stress, and restoring the body to optimal fitness. But it's so much richer if you use it as a spiritual practice, which is what it was originally intended for.

What you see mainly in the West is yoga asana, which is the movement and posture-based practice of yoga. Occasionally you see teachers highlighting the pranayama, but rarely do you find a teacher versed in the Yamas and Nyamas, the codes of living. Most students of yoga who call themselves Yogis and post beautiful pictures all over social media of themselves doing incredible poses don't really understand the spiritual nature of yoga; its meaning has become lost in Ego.

I hear people comment all the time about how much they love yoga – it's so on trend now to be a yogi. Sadly, though, as with many spiritual practices which suddenly gain popularity for only one aspect of them, yoga has lost its true meaning in the West. Sadly, I've heard of those who call themselves yoga teachers and then deny believing in God. I once had a 'yoga teacher' actually say to me that anything connected to God was evil, even saying the only truth is mother nature. She told me she believed herself to be a 'true yogi' but, from what I could see, she didn't fully understand the essence and meaning of yoga if she couldn't see that through yoga you practice stillness and awareness in order to connect with your higher self and, in this connection to your higher self – what I call the True Self – you connect back to God. In my understanding, mother nature is God. Whether God is seen as masculine or feminine, is it still not God?

But in the West, in many yoga classes there's no connection made to God or to the Divine in any capacity – there is only physical exercise. Often there's not even a teaching on consciousness and higher self, nor of love and compassion. It seems instead there are only the postures, and a whole lot of Ego around these postures.

In yoga the breath is integral to mind and body cleansing: breath is life, it's our very life force. Breath is the energy of God moving through you, energising you and bringing you back to stillness so you can feel the presence of God within as you connect to your higher self, your True Self.

To fully embrace the yoga teachings, to channel the discipline to dedicate your life to the practice is to dedicate your life to a spiritual practice, a practice which connects you to God.

This might sound harsh but the truth is, anything else is just exercise and callisthenics.

Yoga is a way of learning to come back to yourself, and truly relax into who you are authentically. The first text of yoga, called the Yoga-Sutra, was written 2500 years ago by Patanjali. In it he defined yoga as 'chitta vritti nirodha', which means the cessation of the 'turnings of the mind': stilling the mind.

Remind you of anything? The same goal as in Buddhism, to release and liberate you from your own mind's torment.

Under is a summary of the Yamas and Niyamas so you can see that yoga is a holistic lifestyle, a spiritual system of living.

In the Sutras, Patanjali outlines the Eight Limbs of Raja Yoga. The first five are exoteric, meaning they are intended to be easily understood by the general population.

They deal with objects outside of oneself, in relation to the body and society. These are Yama (attitudes towards our environment); Niyama (attitudes towards ourselves); Asana (physical postures); Pranayama (restraint or expansion of the breath); and Pratyahara (withdrawal of the senses).

The next three are esoteric, meaning they are intended for a specific, select group of people who would be able to understand and interpret them, integrating them into their lives. These are yoga – Dharana (concentration); Dhyana (meditation); and Samadhi (complete integration).

Because of this, and the nature of this chapter, I'm simply going to focus on the yamas, niyamas, asana, pranayama and pratyahara.

YAMAS

Ahimsa: love, harmlessness, non-killing, non-violence, the absence of harmful intentions, the abandonment of all hostility, even in your own mind. It's a very high degree of consciousness and in many case it is not even achieved by great saints or spiritual teachers, because it also includes not attracting violence towards oneself. Self judgement and beating yourself up is enacting a mental violence against yourself.

Satya: where there is perfected truthfulness the aspirant is said to have developed the power of internal speech – those little voices in your own head. This idea supports the belief that whatever you think comes true. You manifest your thoughts.

It's said that truthfulness starts in knowing and understanding your own mind and then intentionally thinking and speaking each word with spiritual power. Satya is not only refraining from telling lies, but also the ability to see the truth and live it.

Satya tells us that God is truth and can be realised by observing truth in your own thoughts, words and actions.

Asteya: is about being honest. Refrain from stealing. Intentionally recognising the desire to have what doesn't belong to you, then letting that desire go so you don't go doing something you'll later regret.

Brahmacharya: this is my favourite one. Brahmacharya is often confused with refraining from sex, however this is not really true. It's more about conserving our energy and finding balance with this sexual energy so it's spread evenly throughout our lives. It also means we need to take our energy away from external desires and instead direct the energy to internal desires.

Aparigraha: letting go of the need to have lots of material things for external pleasures. Recognise what's greed and let it go.

Learn to recognise what has meaning and what is just filling a temporary gap.

I don't believe you have to get rid of all the lovely things you enjoy. I have a thing for designer shoes, even though I rarely get a chance to wear them. I like to look at them and wear them around the house sometimes, but I've learned to recognise my greed and my need for them to fill a gap in me, born of boredom, fear or lack of self-worth. Again, it goes back to understanding balance and your own mind where truth and fear are concerned.

NIYAMAS

Shaucha: cleanliness or purity, not only of body although it does include this – don't you always feel better after a shower? Shaucha is also cleanliness from bad thoughts or even memories. This is where practising mindfulness to train your mind to be in the present comes in. When you're not weighed down by past of future fears of the Ego mind, you can be more positive and focussed on the here and now.

Keeping a clean and tidy environment also helps the mind to centre. It's this idea which inspires all the 'declutter your environment' coaching and therapies that are springing up today. In psychotherapy we often see that when someone is chaotic on the outside – in their lives, their relationships, their environment – then their mind is also often unfocussed, chaotic and in turmoil too.

As a recent example of this, the other Sunday I was quite unfocussed, my mind racing with worry and unrest. I felt claustrophobic and as if I was being suffocated. This is a personal default setting of mine when I'm stressed and starting to feel overwhelmed. It was so consuming I couldn't think straight enough to see what I needed to do first to get everything done. I felt paralysed by my own mind. Everything in my mind was a jumble. So I took the advice in Niyamas – I focussed on my external environment and started slowly cleaning the bathroom. At first with little enthusiasm but then the more I cleaned the more my mind started to refocus. Soon my energy became more positive and I even started to feel good. Who knew cleaning could be like therapy! I guess that's where the saying comes from about idle hands and idle minds leading to suffering and sin… or something like that!

Santosha: true happiness comes from contentment. Contentment avoids mental complexes such as overthinking things and want, want, wanting for the sake of it. Santosha means being content with what you have, who you are, what you do, and where you are in your life. Now, having said that, you also shouldn't settle for a life that makes you miserable either. Instead, as this book is trying to tell you, you need to figure out who you are, and what you're here to do, and make that your life. Then a longing for temporary fixes of happiness will go and you'll find true and lasting contentment.

Tapas:

> *'A worthy aim makes life illumined, pure and divine.*
> *Without such an aim, action and prayer have no value.*
> *Life without tapas is like a heart without love'* – BKS Iyengar

Tapas asks us to invoke our internal flame (what I call and teach as the Holy Fire) to practice a passionate and disciplined spiritual practice to burn away any obstacles standing in the way of you living a spiritually devoted and authentic life. This is another of my favourites because it reminds me to ignite the Holy Fire inside me daily, to consolidate my understanding of and connection with the Divine. I'm also a Holy Fire Master healer, so this is particularly appropriate in my practice.

Swadhyaya: Know Thyself. This is True Self-awareness through self-observation, closing the eyes and observing your own nature and mind. The study of some form of scripture is often suggested. For me it's A Course in Miracles (which is spiritual psychotherapy), the Gnostic Gospels and Buddhism. However, scripture study and understanding are worthless in the absence of knowing your own True Self.

Become the 'watcher' and the witness of your Ego mind and of your True Self. Have the courage to see your Ego imperfections and often toxic behavioural traits. This is another area where using your journal can be beneficial, but don't beat yourself up. Note your behaviours and move on.

Ishvara Pranidhana: Success comes by complete resignation to God, the ultimate surrender and trust.

It's often the case that you only really surrender when you're in internal anguish or conflict. This is very much like acceptance in the Buddhist Noble Truths and why Buddhists believe through suffering comes wisdom. It's in ultimate surrender that you let go and see the truth – and the bigger picture – of life. I believe the more you surrender, the happier you'll be. That's why there's a whole chapter on surrender later in the book. You also hear of surrender as

'Thy Will Be Done' in the Lord's prayer, which we'll talk a little more about later in this chapter.

Surrender is said to be the most difficult of the yamas and niyamas. One completely lets go of all Ego and surrenders to the Divine and to God. Patanjali did not interpret God as a deity. For him, it's said that God was the unchanging reality behind all manifested things.

Mindfulness Through Prayer, The Way of the Rose, and Christ Consciousness

I grew up with a Catholic mother and a father who described himself as open. I went to a Christian school where we had assembly every day, a space and time for us to be inspired through biblical stories and to sing hymns of praise to God. I always enjoyed our assembly time and loved hearing the stories, where the meaning and lesson was always revealed at the end.

From an early age I remember knowing there is a God and being able to understand the bible teachings, even the stories which were hard for adults to see; I knew the meaning behind them. I never once feared God or felt threatened by Christian religion as I know others have. I've always known that God is love. Even when stories were told of a vengeful or judgemental God, I always knew these stories were just a different interpretation, and that behind such stories lay a deeper meaning.

Part of my purpose in this world is to help others return to God and the Divine by returning to themselves. It's my calling to help others see that the way of Christ was to help you achieve a sense of whole self, an awakened consciousness, so that you live with love. Judgement, fear, sadness – these are not part of God's love. The biggest misconception keeping people in the West trapped in ignorance is our fear of returning to God because of all the negative propaganda we've been given in the past. The words of Jesus Christ have been used to manipulate people to remain trapped in fear and disconnected from their True Selves, whereas the love of God actually sits within them.

This is nothing new. I'm sure by now you've all heard similar, albeit controversial, thoughts from Dan Brown's *The Da Vinci Code*. But some scars run deep – we've had two thousand years of lies, manipulation, torture and oppression from those who claimed they were acting in the name of God. Is it any wonder that when someone mentions Christianity, or the word God, some people have a deep fear and resentment and automatically retract and shut down? I don't blame those who feel this way, but here's what I know to be the truth:

Two thousand years ago Jesus walked this earth and taught wisdom and a way for us to become whole, congruent, loving people, where life had meaning and we lived in a state of inner peace. His message teaching us how to live an authentic life, where we are truly happy, serves the world and all beings. This message was one of love, Divine love, where no one was above or below another.

Jesus wasn't alone. Yes, he had his disciples, but he also had his partner, in spirit and in life: Mary Magdalene. I, and many who follow The Way of the Rose, which is based mainly on the Gnostic gospels and teaching of the Divine feminine, believe Mary Magdalene was Jesus's wife and spiritual equal. She was the Divine feminine representative of God and he the masculine. Together they brought balance in their teachings. Like Ying and Yang, night and day, male and female, the sun and the moon; it's all about balance. One can't exist without the other.

If you want to read further on this subject, see Further Reading at the back of this book. It's my belief Mary Magdalene and her message of inner peace through Divine love was hushed up, removed from history, and she was made out to be a sex worker who Jesus pretty much just felt sorry for.

But there were those who knew the truth and kept her message alive throughout the two thousand years since her lifetime. Such a powerful message of love and feminine strength can never be truly obliterated, and as we feel the tides turning for women, it's no coincidence that her name is being heard more and more, louder and louder. She is rising alongside the Divine feminine. Mary Magdalene's message and the Divine feminine Goddess are rising once again to bring balance back to our world, and, with it, peace and the true teachings and message of Christ.

Again, just like the above systems of spiritual belief and practices, The Way of the Rose is extensive, but I'll keep it short here. As with the other two, you'll see there are overlaps and similarities. Also, The Way of the Rose is not only a celebration of the Magdalene and her feminine archetype, but it's also the path to Christ Consciousness, which means an awareness of the True Self as part of a higher universal system. Christ Consciousness is a state of mind where there's an understanding that there is a universal and omnipresent force around us and inside us all, which connects all beings and nature.

Christ Consciousness is not linked to religious beliefs – it's a state of elevation, one which Jesus achieved when resurrected. We believe, and Jesus taught, that this level of consciousness is inside us all and we all have the ability to achieve it. You don't have to be born special or anointed to priesthood. It's not a religious path, it's a spiritual path of self-awareness, self-mastery, love and light.

The aim is to become more loving, compassionate, tolerant, patient, forgiving, understanding and content, by following a new way of conscious thinking; the means by which one achieves this are not important. Remind you of anything above? Just a side note, many believe Jesus, Jesus Christ was also a Yogi… Just saying…

To achieve Christ Consciousness, you grow spiritually by aligning with your authentic True Self through your inner thoughts and feelings.

It's this understanding which embedded my spiritual practice and helped it emanate from my heart and not just from my mind. I became dedicated to seeing and experiencing the world through Divine love in conjunction with self-awareness, mindfulness and compassion. This really accelerated my inner growth and got rid of some pretty toxic demons which were stopping me from fully embracing my purpose and all the possibilities of what my life could and should be.

It's the practice of The Way of the Rose which gave me the courage to live authentically, attuned to my True Self, and to say out loud that my belief in God and the Divine and the daily practice and dedication to this path is why I'm so successful and happy with my life. It helped me get past my deep-rooted fear of being seen and feeling shame and embarrassment because of my dyslexia and always feeling like the 'stupid one' in the room.

And this is my intention throughout this book: to help you start on your own path to your Christ Consciousness, in whatever way you feel called to do it, on whatever path feels right for you.

When you follow The Way of the Rose you are following a path to consciously transform and heal your own mind and heart through self-compassion, compassion to others and Divine love, through connecting back to your Soul, which is your True Self, and ultimately back to God.

As we've talked about in earlier chapters, one of the most toxic tricks your Ego plays is to make your greatest dreams feel like your greatest fears. It's a cruel game of control to keep you oppressed and the Ego strong. It tells you that you can't answer the call to your purpose because you're tired, unqualified, unworthy, broke... and anyway, you just don't have the time.

The Way of the Rose is a path to achieve Christ Consciousness and has many facets. The practice I'm going to concentrate on here is the Lord's prayer.

When you follow the path of The Way of the Rose you follow the teachings of the Magdalene and Jesus, through the Lord's prayer, to release you from the torment of the Ego which blinds you.

As with all the above spiritual practices and teachings, this is just a brief summary, but a good summary to use for insight.

The Lord's Prayer

The Lord's Prayer encompasses everything you need to know about the teachings of Jesus and the Magdalene: 'The Way of Truth for those with eyes to see'. Not many people realise, and this included me for a long time, that the prayer was given to us directly from Jesus himself when asked by his disciples to teach them how to pray.

Jesus gave this prayer as an affirmation of truth. Truth about ourselves, our potential, our purpose, who we are in this world, why we're here, and our connection to God. It's not meant to be said by rote, but instead said consciously and reflectively. Understanding and meaning each word you say, linking it to your life and state of mind at the time in that moment. The Lord's Prayer is an affirmation and the most powerful of them all. Like any affirmation or mantra, it's the energy you put into the words from your heart that gives the affirmation meaning, purpose and power.

Seeing the Prayer Clearly for the First Time

'Our Father'

Let's get this first bit cleared up right now, shall we, because I already suspect what you may be thinking here after two thousand years of manipulation... so, let's be clear: Jesus did not use the word Father so we would imagine a fearful, judgemental old man sitting on a throne condemning us for our mistakes. He used it to describe a Divine parent representative of both male and female

Divinity and love akin to parental love. To make this clear, I like to use Mother-Father God.

Think of the love you feel for your child – this is the unconditional message of love portrayed here through these opening words to the prayer.

'Who Art In Heaven'

This is to signify that God is an omniscient (all knowing and all wise), omnipresent (all around us and inside us), and omnipotent (all powerful; the ultimate authority) Universal being.

Our spiritual parent Mother-Father God is always with us, surrounding us with love, compassion, kindness and generosity (note there's no judgement of fear here). There's nothing our Mother-Father God would not do for us if we help ourselves in opening our hearts to Him-Her spiritually and aligning with our True Selves to bring heaven to earth.

'Hallowed Be Thy Name'

Hallowed is an ancient Aramaic word, which was the language of Jesus in his time. It means 'to set apart' – in this case, for the purpose of adoration and reverence. God is omnipresent, a formless light and Divine energy. To hallow His-Her name is to open our hearts to the space within us and in our lives, and allow Him-Her to fill it with Divine love.

Your heart centre and heart chakra are where the Holy Fire sits within you waiting to be ignited. This is the true 'church' and it sits already inside you. This is why Jesus said, 'Where your heart is, there your treasure is also.'

To place God in the centre of your heart is to devote everything you say and do to love. This includes your thoughts and feelings towards yourself. A Course in Miracles tells us, 'You are a work of God, and His work is wholly lovable and wholly loving. This is how you must come to think of yourself in your heart, because this is what you are.'

'Thy Kingdom Come, Thy Will Be Done, On Earth As It Is In Heaven'

When Jesus said, 'Behold, the kingdom of heaven is inside you,' – that famous quote I'm sure you must have heard – he also said, in the Gospel of Thomas, 'The Kingdom of heaven is spread out upon the earth, but man does not see it.' Jesus is telling us to awaken to the truth of the present moment. Heaven is not when you're dead, the Kingdom of heaven is now. Wake up and reconnect to God by living through your True Self, which knows only love. Let this Divine love emanate from you into the world so that it is on earth as it is in heaven.

Start by making time for you, reconnect to your True Self, let go of the fear of the Ego mind and reconnect to the Divine love of God, then share this love with the world to heal and restore peace.

'And Give Us This Day Our Daily Bread'

With this line Jesus isn't referring to the bread we eat. Certainly not the bread of today with all its toxins and artificial preservatives, that's for sure.

Jesus is referring to spiritual food for thought: for inspiration and our spiritual nourishment, our daily need for teachings, inspiration, loving thoughts to inspire Christ Consciousness and the experience of God's love. This is what we need to practice daily to keep us from getting consumed once again by the terror of the Ego mind's control and oppression through disconnection and distraction.

Every day we should be returning to our heart centre to practice prayer, meditation and reflection in whatever way inspires and speaks to us most, to keep us connected to our True Selves and God's love.

'And Forgive Us Our Trespasses, As We Forgive Those Who Trespass Against Us'

First, note here that I use trespasses and trespass, but you may have heard the word debt and debtors, which is an older version of the prayer. I've always been taught trespasses, so this resonates with me more, but feel free to use debt and debtors if that is what you've been taught. It means the same thing.

Through this line of the prayer we're being taught that only through forgiveness can we ever truly be set free. While you hold grudges, unforgiveness, resentment and grievances in your heart there can't be love. Such things only come from the Ego and fear. The word trespass or debt refers to judgement, grievances, anger, resentment and envy.

To not forgive is to split yourself off from the source of love; there's no room in your heart and mind for love if it is full of grievances caused by fear.

'And Lead Us Not Into Temptation But Deliver Us From Evil'

To understand this line of the prayer you must remember that 1) the language used in the time it was written can perhaps be a little dramatic, hence the word 'evil'; and 2) to understand the first part of the line 'And lead us not into temptation', you must look to the second part 'but deliver us from evil'.

You must also remember that any action or thought which instils fear in us comes from the Ego mind and separates us or disconnects us from God's love. This Ego mind, this human fear, is what is being referred to as evil. Our Ego mind and the fear and disconnection from the truth are our internal demons.

No matter what fears and negative self-sabotaging emotions and behaviours we experience as a result of the Ego, if we are prepared to intentionally surrender these to God, and return to our True Selves through meditation, reflection and prayer, we can give all these evils back to God for healing and transformation. We don't have to carry the weight and burden of them, we just have to intentionally take responsibility for understanding them as a part of us and our projection out on to the world, and then let them go through surrender, trust and faith.

'For Thine Is The Kingdom, The Power And The Glory For Ever'

The prayer ends with us being reminded that God is omnipresent and is inside each and every one of us in every moment of each blessed day we have the opportunity to connect with His-Her Love. There is no need for fear – everything the Ego mind offers is an illusion. We take the opportunity at the end of the prayer to reinforce our commitment to opening our hearts and awakening to our True Selves to reconnect to God, to the only truth and the true power. In the glory that is for ever for those who believe and are willing to see, nothing is impossible.

'Amen'

To me, all the above spiritual practices say the same thing. Inner peace and ultimate happiness can be found when you intentionally choose to open your heart and mind to believing in something bigger than you. When you choose to understand that you are a spiritual being having a human experience, and that by choosing to connect back to your spiritual True Self you can not only make yourself happy and heal and transform your own life, you will transform the lives of your children and community; even the world.

As far as I'm concerned, The Lord's Prayer tells us everything we need to know about connecting with God. Most of the Bible is man-made and colludes with the Ego.

I, and many like me, believe the true words of Jesus and the Magdalene unfortunately got abused; it's a strong word but sadly fitting. Because of this, millions upon millions have paid the price of the collective Ego.

To believe in God, or to have a spiritual practice and to understand your deepest fears and insecurities, takes a higher level of emotional intelligence and leads to strength, not to an oppressed weakness.

My greatest wish, as a woman, as a mother and as a human being, is that you return to your True Self and see how much more you can contribute to the world than you do when you are hiding, afraid of judgement, and experiencing the pain caused by living an inauthentic life. Those patterns repeat themselves in our children. For many women, the greatest gift is becoming a mother. Children are their strength, their mirrors and their greatest teachers.

To help share a little more about how I practise the Lord's Prayer, I'm going to introduce you to the Labyrinth and the Seven Chakras.

The Labyrinth

The Chakra System, the Lord's Prayer and the Walk to Inner Peace

If you haven't ever seen or heard of a labyrinth, these are ancient, complex, circular maze-like pathways which were designed to be walked as a way of reflection, meditation and prayer. They're believed to date back roughly 5000 years and obviously pre-date Christianity.

Walking the labyrinth is believed to be a sacred walk into the centre of True Self with one way in and one way out. This is what makes a labyrinth (unicursal) different to a maze (multicursal). The labyrinth has one entrance, one exit and is designed to have one path, whereas a maze has multiple paths, exits, entrances and dead ends. A maze leads to further confusion. A labyrinth is a meditative tool for inner clarity and peace.

There are many variations of labyrinths, the oldest and the one considered to be the classic labyrinth is associated with the famous Greek legend of King Minos of Knossos in Crete. The labyrinth represents our personal journey through our human experience: we encounter many twists and turns that may detour us but there's only one path. In this case, with the classic labyrinth, there are seven circuits (in others there can be four or eleven), and each one of these circuits represents the seven chakras.

In case you're not familiar with chakras, these are energy centres which sit within the body; the seven main ones travel alongside your spine. When your chakras are out of balance it means there is imbalance in your mind, body and spirit. Clearing toxic energy and bringing in new clean energy from the Divine is an essential practice to ensure good emotional, physical and of course spiritual health.

This is how I consciously use the labyrinth to pray, meditate, channel and find my way back to myself and to God when I feel lost or stressed out.

It's not part of my daily practice because labyrinths, believe it or not, are not as common as churches. However, I do make it a priority to walk one at least several times of year. My favourite is in Chartres, in France, but my regular practice labyrinth is in Glastonbury, in the UK. If you wanted to try this practice out you could download a copy online and follow the path with your finger. This is known as a finger labyrinth and was quite common in medieval times as they were built into church walls for pilgrims to use, when bigger ones people could walk weren't available.

There's so much history to the use of labyrinths for spiritual practice that I could write a whole book dedicated to the subject, but I won't go in-depth here. See the Further Reading section at the back of the book if you want to learn more, or look on YouTube. As with everything else, there's a tonne of good videos demonstrating how to use a labyrinth and giving you more history about their origins.

When I walk the labyrinth I'm surrendering to the Divine, bringing energy in through my chakras and praying for wisdom. I'm consciously setting my intention to raise my level of inner awareness and my consciousness, and embody Divine love. It's a truly beautiful practice and experience and one that's easy to add to your own spiritual practice.

Below is a brief explanation of the seven main chakras and how they relate to the seven circuits of the labyrinth.

Labyrinth and Chakra Exercise

The walk entails completing a full circuit of the labyrinth for each Chakra.

Step into the labyrinth and begin your prayer and reflective journey at the Root Chakra. The Root Chakra sits at the base of the spine, is a deep red in colour and its element is earth. Its energy helps us feel grounded, connected to the earth and in balance.

The second circuit in the labyrinth is symbolic of the second Chakra, the Sacral Plexus. Its colour is orange and its element is water. This is where our sexual and creative energy lies, along with our ability to connect with our emotions and with others. Your Sacral Chakra sits roughly two inches (about 5 cm) below your navel.

The third Chakra and circuit of the labyrinth is the Solar Plexus. Its colour is yellow and its element is fire. Its energy is related to our self-confidence, acceptance and our ability to value ourselves. It sits in the belly near the lowest rib.

The fourth Chakra is the Heart Chakra. It is green in colour and is connected to the element of air. Its energy is connected with self, compassion, love, forgiveness and empathy.

The fifth Chakra is the Throat Chakra. Its colour is blue and its element is earth and ether. Its energy is connected to self-expression and the ability to speak your truth. Its location is in the throat.

The sixth Chakra is the Third Eye Chakra. Its colour is indigo and its element is water; its energy is connected with intuition and clairvoyance. Its location is on the forehead, between the eyes.

Finally, the seventh Chakra and circuit in the labyrinth is the Crown Chakra. Its colour is purple and its element is fire. Its energy is connected directly with God and the Divine. When you connect with God and the Divine you channel energy down through your Crown Chakra, so it can flow and reinvigorate and balance the other chakras;

this energy comes directly from Source. You also channel energy up through the Root Chakra, which comes from the energy of the earth. It flows up through all other chakras and leaves through the Crown Chakra, returning to Source, God and the Divine, thereby connecting heaven and earth. On its way through it ignites the Holy Spirit and Holy Fire within you. This is the gift that Jesus talked about already being inside us. When this energy flows through you and your Chakras are in total balance you are embodying the Divine and uniting heaven and earth within you!

Isn't that beautiful? This is your gift: your ability to heal yourself, to bring balance back, to reconnect to your True Self, work through the various levels of consciousness and achieve inner peace.

As you've seen, mindfulness is at the core of all the above practices, and it can stand alone. As a form of psychology, mindfulness is good at helping you manage issues such as anxiety and stress. However, when practised as a spiritual practice its true healing capacity is absorbed. Whatever you choose to believe, practising mindfulness meditation every day for at least 20 minutes per day will bring about lasting emotional and physical health benefits.

Below is a simple sitting breath mindfulness meditation. I practise this every day for 30 minutes, sometimes more, and sometimes twice a day. It has made a huge difference in my ability to manage feelings of being overwhelmed, feelings of anxiety and doubt, and emotional outbursts, especially during that ladies' time of the month. Its psychological and neurological benefits are enormous. Again, for further information check out the recommended reading section at the back of the book. I highly recommend that, if nothing else reaches you in this book, you commit to practising the exercise below for at least 20 minutes per day. Believe me when I say your future self will thank you for it, as will your children, and your children's children. A good solid mindfulness meditation daily practice literally rewires your brain, it's that life changing!

Sitting Breath Mindfulness Meditation

You can read this practice through and repeat it, or you can go to my website aimeeleighsmith.com and download my free audio mp3 meditation guiding you through the practice.

Make yourself comfortable, remove yourself from distractions, anoint yourself with essential oils – try the recipe below or one of the others if you prefer. Practise this sitting mindfulness meditation for 20 minutes.

Begin by coming to sit quietly, gently close your eyes and tune into your breath.

Take three long, slow, deep breaths, breathing in fully and exhaling fully. Breathe in through your nose and out through your nose or mouth. Then allow your breath to find its own natural rhythm.

Now bring your full attention to noticing each in-breath as it enters your nostrils, travels down to your lungs and causes your belly to expand. Notice each out-breath as your belly contracts and air moves up through the lungs, back up through the nostrils or mouth. Concentrate your full attention to flow with your breath.

Now begin to let go of any noises around you. If you are distracted by sounds in or outside the room, just notice them and then focus your intention back on your breath.

Try to just breathe. Don't try to control or change anything about your breath.

Try to observe and accept your experience in this moment without judgement, paying attention to each inhale and exhale. If your mind wanders to thoughts, plans or problems, simply notice your mind wandering.

If your mind has wandered, bring your attention back to your breath. Your breath is an anchor you can return to over and over again when you become distracted by thoughts. Observe the types of thoughts that distract you. Becoming aware of the kind of thoughts that distract you can strengthen your ability to detach from these thoughts in the moment of practice and in your day-to-day life.

Acknowledge whatever comes up in your practice, including thoughts or stories about your experiences. Simply notice where your mind goes without judging it, pushing it away, clinging to it or wishing it were different.

Journalling Exercise

Knowing all you know about the above spiritual beliefs and practices, open up your journal and ask yourself how you feel about them. Which ones do you resonate with? Is there one more than another? For example, do you prefer the Eightfold Path? Or walking the labyrinth, or meditating on your chakras?

What does this mean to you? How is it making you now see yourself and your relationship to the Divine or God? Is there an aspect that still sits uncomfortably with you. If so, why?

Can you see and understand the importance of heart-felt intention in your mindfulness practice or your spiritual practice? Has this experience ignited your experience and sense of Divine love within, bringing about a deeper understanding of faith, trust and peace?

For me, having faith, trust and Divine love in my heart brings about a focussed inner peace and belief in myself, which brings a deep gratitude and joy for my life. Also, during those days when I feel overwhelmed it makes me let go and give the stress of it all back to God; it's like taking a heavy backpack off and breathing a sigh of relief. But how does it make you feel? This is the most crucial question.

Use the essential oil recipe below to inspire and deepen your spiritual reflection. These oils will hold you as you open your heart and let go of any beliefs that no longer serve your highest good.

Essential Oils Recipe

For deep reflection, blend:

Rose: is the highest vibrating oil and connects you directly to Divine love. Rose essential oil is considered to be a sacred oil and helps with opening the Heart Chakra and strengthening your ability to feel compassion towards yourself and others, and to express love.

Frankincense: again, this essential oil connects you with the Divine and helps you speak and live your truth. It's wonderful to use when meditating and channelling new energy to cleanse the Chakras.

Sandalwood: is grounding, relaxing and calming. It helps you ground deep into the energy of the earth so you feel rooted and connected to your True Self and have a good sense of mental clarity.

Amaris: is for focus and concentration, to keep you tuned into your breath and the present moment.

6

Surrender and Acceptance

*'The moment of surrender is not when
life ends, it's when it begins'*
— Marianne Williamson

The first big misconception I need to address right away in this chapter is that surrender and acceptance are not a form of weakness. They are courageous choices that take immense clarity, vision and trust in the Divine.

To surrender is not to just give up. It is a way to reignite feelings of hope and love.

When you consciously choose to surrender, you're choosing to step out of your own way and give your Self back to God to guide you in whatever way is the best way for all beings. To do this in our culture today, in a world and society that's driven by fear, is so very, very powerful. Part of what keeps you disconnected and distracted from your True Self and living an in-authentic life is the Ego telling you that you have control and if you feel you don't then you must take it back no matter the cost, even if the cost is to your health and your relationships.

This is also very much a collective Ego belief, which fuels our current crisis of stress and poor mental and physical health.

This forced belief system runs through every part of your life, your partner's, your relationships with your children, your relationship with your business and your relationship with yourself.

So much of our time today as women, mothers, partners and friends is spent trying to control everything. Trying to be the best organiser, or fixer. When your child falls over, the first thing you instinctively do is want to try and fix their pain, to take it away even. The Ego mind would have us believe that we can indeed control everything in our lives, even down to how our children feel and function in the world. But we can't, and when you try to control everything, or believe you can, you're colluding with the Ego and resisting the Divine from working through you.

Understanding surrender and acceptance is the cornerstone of any spiritual practice. It is when you can understand that you exist in this world to be a teacher and a server of the Divine – which we all are, we all have this inside us, especially when we become mothers and carers of children. This is why the journey of womanhood is so vital to creating a conscious society for tomorrow. As a woman in our society you're often the most real spiritual teacher your children will have.

When you can understand and embrace this role and call to womanhood, you can see how vital it is that you continue with whatever spiritual practice you choose. You're not alone, the Divine loves you also. As the Divine worked through you to nourish your body to empower you to grow and nurture life, the Divine is also gifting you with this same growth.

Rather than bearing the weight of responsibility and being a rescuer, let the Divine work through you to teach you with universal wisdom.

Motherhood isn't just those who have borne children, being a mother is when you create, nurture and nourish from your heart. This can be towards children, and often is, but it's also towards the earth and towards yourself and your own dreams.

Let's keep exploring how surrendering to the Divine, to an energy and power that's bigger than us can lead to the ultimate peace and serenity.

Controlling Others

Have you ever heard yourself thinking, or even saying, 'He just won't do what I tell him to!' Or do you find yourself slyly trying to change your children or partner, disappointed in who they are, and eventually it becomes your mission to try and control and change them?

Or are you a rescuer? Is it unbearable for you to see your children suffering, so you have to take charge and rescue them from their situation?

I can relate to all of the above. My husband is a very different person to me, and he practices his spirituality in a very different way to me. Sometimes I see him suffering with an issue with a friend or family member and I know some meditation, or a consistent practice of prayer each day would help him see and experience the world differently. I used to nag him into joining me on my path, and it just caused further resistance. I would get cross and huffy, insisting I knew what was best for him and taking it personally that he wouldn't listen to me, especially when I thought I was right! Even with issues such as keeping up his supplements and essential oil intake to keep his immunity and health strong. Sometimes, he just wouldn't do it, he wouldn't listen to me and thought he knew best. Until one day he came home with a raging flu. I realised I could say 'I told you so' – and I did.

But what I found in all these situations – and trust me, there are more stories I could tell – was that the more I pushed him and tried to insist I knew best and that my way was the right way, the more he fought against me.

It took time for me to realise he has his own path, he has his own spiritual self to find, and his own lessons to learn. His journey is his in every possible sense or scenario you can think of.

We do it with our children as well, right? They fall down, we rush to pick them up; they're slow at reading, we blame ourselves; they're getting bullied and it crushes us because the feelings of helplessness at not being able to save them is too much to bear. You get pushy parents that cajole and bully their children into perceived success or being 'better', because of their need to control and feel they're in charge of constructing this world around them.

Let me tell you a paradoxical little secret, though: you *are* in charge of creating your world. You absolutely are what you think, and your actions have a cause-and-effect energy. But trying to push and force anything in your life will only cause you pain, because you're attached to the idea that you actually have any control. And you don't. That's the paradox: you create it, but you're not in control of it.

If you want to create the life you're meant to live, the one you dream of, you must surrender and let the Divine work through you. You must commit to surrendering and letting go of attachment and Ego, so that you hear your True Self speak and guide you. Your Ego will only lead you to further attachment, further struggle and a feeling that you have to control everything. And that if something happens outside of your control then it's likely to be a disaster. Isn't that exhausting!

One of my clients (call her Beth for the sake of her anonymity), spent her childhood moving from foster care home to women's refuge. Nothing felt stable in her life, ever; she never knew whether she was coming or going. As a result, her Ego mind developed this self-protective need to control everything she did. This grew as she became an adult and her choices regarding her life became her own. So, she unconsciously developed these controlling behavioural traits, where she would plan everything down to the last detail, and when life happened, or people – for example, her husband and children – didn't adhere to her perfectly constructed plan, she would flip out. Her anxiety was through the roof and her emotional outbursts were completely irrational to everyone around her. The more fraught life became with the usual challenges such as job hunts or schooling issues, the more she tried to control the people and events around her, the more stressed she got and the more disillusioned, fearful and angry she became when things didn't work out according to this perfect picture in her mind. By the time we started working together, her marriage was all but over and her daughter had taken on many of these behaviours, too, which were presenting as anxiety and regressive, childlike behavioural symptoms.

Beth originally came to me for help with her daughter because of the anxiety. This is often the case – the symptom that's recognisable presents itself and the person thinks they just need to learn a little cognitive technique to manage it. Our whole psychology system is based on putting a bandage on the problem. However, through working together I was able to help Beth see that the chaos in the home, the breakdown of her marriage and her daughter's response to this all stemmed from her own painful, fearful childhood and the Ego mind, which now dominated her every decision and life choice.

Helping Beth see this, as hopefully this book will help you come to recognise your own behaviours, helped her understand the need to surrender and let go of her need to control. As a child she wasn't in control, her parents were, the care services were, this is why she tried to protect herself by controlling everything and everyone around her whenever she could. When those things felt like they were slipping away or not in her control, the fear was so strong she literally couldn't think straight! And she became so far removed from her True Self, all hell literally broke loose in her mind.

I worked with Beth to understand this Ego-driven behaviour pattern, teaching her to have some self-compassion because what she endured as a child was devastating and was still the cause of her suffering. She's human, she needs to forgive herself for her perceived mistakes. Then

I was able to help Beth, through meditation and prayer, to practice surrendering to the Divine. Inviting the Holy spirit (Universe, if you prefer, or God, as I do) to enter through her.

You have to make the choice to wake up and recognise your own Ego mind, and to make your own connection with the Divine. Once you make that choice and commit to a daily practice of prayer and surrender, life isn't such a scary place. Liberation and peace come from surrender. The unrealistic burden of you being the one to have to fix everything and make everything in your life work is released and lifted from your shoulders.

Surrender is Not a Weakness

Just as compassion isn't indulgent, surrender isn't a weakness. Many people, when they first commit to learning about and understanding the meaning and concept of surrender, initially feel it's a way of giving up. But surrender is anything but a weakness or giving up. Learning to surrender and trust in a source greater than yourself takes immense courage. Committing to a daily practice where you apply the principles of surrender to your life takes discipline and dedication. Does that sound like giving up, or a thing of weakness to you?

Often, when people are consumed by the suffering of the Ego mind, they take on the role of the victim, telling themselves this is all happening *to* them, and that there's nothing they can do. It's happening to them and it's everyone else's fault. Another reaction is, 'This is happening and I'm so weak I can't do anything about it, therefore I'm just going to wallow in my own sense of failure.'

Understanding surrender and acceptance is key to avoiding burnout and getting in the way of your True Self teaching you how to let God flow through you.

The only true power, which comes from the True Self, is surrender and of course love. To surrender is to love and to trust implicitly that you're taken care of. If you can do that, you'll know true peace and the feeling of stress in your life, family, relationship, business – whatever – will be a thing of your past, leaving you free to simply enjoy what you do.

It's important to point out here that you have free will to choose which path you take, and which wolf you feed: love or the Ego mind's fear.

You have the free will to get out of your own way and stop trying to 'control' and fight your way to success.

You have the free will to choose to commit to a daily practice which teaches how to choose love instead of fear and how to get to know your Ego mind, to get out of your own way and surrender to guidance and understand that the weight of your business, family, relationship or children doesn't have to be borne by you alone. In fact, giving it back to God is not only liberating, it's wise because your life will flow where it's naturally meant to go in the direction that's best for you and all beings. When this happens, trust me, it'll flow in wonderful ways you often can't imagine possible for you.

Understanding and practising surrender is key to living in flow and alignment, but I know it doesn't come easy. This is why every day it's important to remind yourself through having a reflective practice which includes prayer and meditation.

When I was going through my dark night, I only began to emerge when I stopped fighting it, when I let go, fell to my knees and prayed for the strength to get out of my own way and let God's love work through me. As I let go of the constant questioning and need to control, my mood began to shift and the dark mists blocking my vision began to clear. When I prayed for love to re-enter my heart so I could receive His guidance once again, I fell silent long enough to hear the guidance coming through.

Prior to my dark night I was running around pushing, striving and attaching to the fight to make my dreams possible. I had this very common unconscious belief that if I wasn't social media famous and raking in the cash, I wasn't successful.

I had lost my vision and any meaning I'd had to the call in the first place.

This is so easy to do living in a world where Ego reigns supreme.

You receive the call, but then your individual inner challenges come, and the real 'work' begins. For me, this was to practise everything I preached and taught.

The Way of the Rose and the true understanding of Christ Consciousness is that there is no teacher above a student; every teacher is a student and every student is a teacher. You teach to learn about yourself and your purpose as much as to teach, help or lead others in understanding theirs. It's all part of serving God, the Divine and others in the name of love and for the good of all beings.

Surrendering allows you to receive as well as give the teaching.

If this is blocked with an 'I already know everything' belief, you're getting in your own way and allowing Ego to control you once again. This way of thinking and feeling is just fear packaged up as a fake illusion of confidence and arrogance.

Acceptance

Acceptance is slightly different to surrender in that surrender is all about letting go, whereas you cultivate a sense of acceptance in choosing to do that. So, for example, in my own story I had to bring a realisation and sense of acceptance to my dark night at that point in my life in order to choose to surrender. When I talk about surrender and acceptance many view them as one, but for me they are two different states of mind and intention, but one is necessary to invoke the other.

In Buddhism the practice of acceptance is paramount to the cessation, the 'end' of suffering. First you must accept the idea that all suffering comes from 'attachment'. When you're able to accept this truth you can work on letting go of your attachment to all things and release yourself from suffering.

I see attachment as clinging, striving, pushing and forcing. If you accept any of these as the cause of your suffering, you can surrender to letting go of the attachment and, as we've discussed, the need to control everything – which is also a form of attachment.

Trust

So, you've heard the call, and you're on your spiritual path, disciplined and ready to answer the call to your purpose and serve others. But then, nothing…

You're stuck! Something is blocking you from taking inspired action. You've followed the first steps of the book, your journal is growing, you've learned about yourself and are really understanding the difference between your Ego and your True Self, you're practising self-compassion and are committed to being present in the moment. Yet something is still missing?

I gave a talk around the time of writing this book at an event for healers and holistic therapists.

Every person in the room was running their own business and committed to living an authentic life, sharing their gifts. They all believed in Spirit and had committed spiritual practices to keep them on their path, yet they struggled to get clients and grow their businesses and make their dreams a reality.

Why?

It wasn't because their social media strategy wasn't up-to-date, or their blogging or marketing plan wasn't quite cutting edge. There was a block and it wasn't external to them; it never really is. Your blocks are always lack of faith and lack of trust. Our biggest blocks are the lack of faith in ourselves and in the Divine to support us in manifesting and following our path. If you lack faith and trust in yourself, then you lack it in God; and if you lack it in God then you'll undoubtedly lack it within yourself.

One of my biggest challenges is a fear of being seen. All

that comes down to is trust and trusting my work and my purpose enough to put it out there, and once again surrender it all up and say, 'Whatever happens, I trust everything will go in the best way possible not only for the good of myself, but of all beings.'

Do you trust God is walking beside you? Do you believe in something bigger than yourself? Do you believe your purpose and path is aligned with this something, with God?

It's scary to make yourself vulnerable and put yourself out on the edge to be seen. But it's necessary if you want to grow. To really put yourself out there, you have to trust that it's going to be ok, that other judgements aren't going to affect you, that you can embrace the difficult times for the lessons they'll teach you, just as much as you can embrace the joy of your accomplishments and of your dreams coming true.

This fear of being seen and judged is your Ego and the collective Ego getting in your way and trying to hold you back and keep you in a place of 'safety', where no one can hurt your feelings or harm you again. It's your deepest fears and limiting beliefs holding you back.

For this reason, trust is an absolute requirement to surrendering, accepting and getting out of your own way and creating a life that serves all beings for the higher good. Trust in something higher than yourself, something pure that unites and guides us all. Set your intention to practise absolute trust and belief. This sense of trust will fuel your ability to surrender and accept. This is the path to less stress and more inner peace.

Do the following meditation exercise to begin to understand where you're attaching, controlling and blocking yourself from moving forward. Your journal may also help you here as you may already have identified certain things you do to sabotage yourself. Following the meditation, practise the prayer for surrender, acceptance and trust to get out of your own way.

Meditation Exercise for Focus

Find a quiet space or go into your meditation area. Use essential oils to ground you and magnify this still practice. Frankincense is a wonderful grounding oil and creates a deeper connection to the Divine.

Spend 20 minutes practising the Sitting Breath Mindfulness Meditation from Chapter 5, to centre and prepare yourself.

Then focus on where you may be attaching, controlling and/ or blocking yourself from moving forward. Avoid judgement. Remember all you've learned about self compassion and self forgiveness.

Prayer for Surrender, Acceptance and Trust

'I pray to see where I'm standing in my own way attaching to an outcome and trying to control, push and strive. I see and accept my fears as part of me, but not all of me. I choose love and consciously let go of all fear-based limits keeping me stuck.

I pray to be guided on my path, and I surrender and trust 'Thy Will Be Done' for the good of all beings.'

Essential Oil Recipe

To magnify this practice and prayer, and strengthen your courage to fully accept, surrender, and trust, blend:

Wintergreen: the essential oil of emotional and physical surrender. As you let go and surrender emotionally, you release tension from your body, in particular around your neck and shoulders.

Neroli: the essential oil of peace and wholeness. Neroli nurtures and rejuvenates your Heart Chakra, helping to relieve anxiety, stress and depression.

Myrrh: to deeply understand the spiritual meaning of struggling and attachment which lead to emotional suffering.

Spikenard: the oil of gratitude. This essential oil cultivates a deep sense of trust by supporting you to appreciate all your life's experiences. Through this appreciation you're fully able to understand how to let go, surrender and accept life exactly as it is.

7

The Power of Gratitude

'The roots of all goodness lie in the soil of
appreciation of all goodness' – Dali Lama

We have a practice in my house: every day when we sit down to eat our family dinner, we each individually say what we're thankful for.

It's our form of family prayer and a way for my husband and I to teach our children the most basic, most important and easiest spiritual practice, but the most profound and often life shifting.

In the morning when I've completed my journalling I always write at least five things that I'm gratful for. It sets me up for the day.

This is so powerful because it's really easy to focus on what you don't have instead of seeing and being grateful for what you do have.

Did you know your brain holds on to the negative more than the positive? Believe it or not, it's a form of self-protection... that's the Ego again. Neurologically, as you learned in the chapter on mindfulness, it's the fight or flight system in action. Also, as you learned, it can be changed with a daily mindfulness practice, so it makes sense for this chapter to come after the mindfulness chapter because incorporating a practice of gratitude into your day-to-day life super charges your mindfulness practice!

It's an instant mood and energy changer which helps you go from deep in the pits of self-pity and hopelessness to boundless energy of hope, optimism and a deep feeling of love.

If your mindset, for whatever reason, is inclined more towards a depressive state, where you often only see the bad in situations, this practice is particularly powerful to help you shift your mental state and thinking patterns to more genuinely positive ones. By truly reflecting on what's good in your life right now – and there's always something – you are *feeling* gratitude, as well as thinking about it. Remember, mindfulness starts with the heart… always!

When you take the time to practise gratitude in an intentional, mindful way, you have a direct experience of being connected to all of life. Often, this comes with the profound understanding that there is more at play than you initially allowed yourself to see, feel and experience. There's more to life's bigger picture. Having a dedicated spiritual practice, which incorporates mindfulness and conscious awareness, elevates you above the low vibrational egoic needs and greeds. It's also a relief to step back from your life's constant drama – even if the respite is only temporary, it's liberating.

Through cultivating a deep and honest sense of thankfulness for all the many wonderful things in your

131

life – even just being alive – helps you tap into a sense of feeling truly blessed and loved. If you feel blessed and loved, you'll start to feel a need to share this love and generosity with other beings, which of course creates further joy and further gratitude. Can you see how this swirls around in a never-ending loop of bliss?

Gratitude and Forgiveness

Gratitude also lays the path for forgiveness because if your heart is full of joy and love, there's no room for holding on to old toxic patterns of anger, resentment or negative energy. Fostering gratitude helps you have more clarity to see things as they are because your heart isn't clouded with toxic energy and feelings.

To be able to forgive yourself and others, or anyone you feel has trespassed against you, is the greatest spiritual achievement and is the foundation for inner peace. It's the greatest weapon – for want of a better word – we have against our inner demons and our Ego, and for bringing about world change. And it all starts with gratitude.

Gratitude is Not About Living in Denial

Throughout my work in mental health services I've met some wonderful people who have been locked in a state of terror and Ego because of truly awful life events and traumas, and as a result have long-standing chronic and often debilitating mental health issues, which really make it difficult for them to see anything good in their lives.

Sometimes when you've had challenge upon challenge thrown at you it can be hard for you to find the positive in any situation to feel grateful for. Life just feels against you and it's a struggle to understand how anyone can ask you to find something to be grateful for.

So, let me be clear here, the practice of moment-to-moment gratitude is not in any way a denial of life's difficulties, stresses, pain or uncertainties. It is a way to rebalance your experience of the world from a bad and negative place, to a good and positive one. It's a way of shifting your feelings, not just papering over the cracks by forcing 'positive thoughts' on yourself repetitively but never really feeling them and then wondering why nothing changes in your life.

Your Brain Holds on to the Bad Stuff More Than the Good Stuff

As I've mentioned, your brain holds on to the negative you see around you and the good and positive falls away. This is a fact. It's a way for your brain to protect you. Anything perceived as bad or threatening is noted and held on to so that if and when it comes up again, you'll be ready for it in case it's a threat. The good stuff isn't perceived as a threat so is just let go; there's no need to make a long-term note of it. Trouble is, with the bombardment of stress and modern-day challenges, the brain is making a lot of mental notes about perceived threats and, as a result, over-whelm and chronic stress happens. Everything seems negative and, with your brain literally holding on to the negative, it's tough for you to see any positive. This makes it all the more important to start a daily gratitude practice.

You need to start training your brain to feel grateful for the good, then you'll see and experience more of it.

To quote a passage from the Bible, the disciple Paul instructs, 'In everything, give thanks.' What he means by this is that from our limited perspective it's not possible to know the outcome of any event or situation in our lives. What can seem at first like bad luck or a negative experience may turn out to be an unexpected blessing. It goes back to my saying 'God gives us what we need and not what we think we want'.

Learning to Trust and Surrender to this way of being and living, and being grateful for whatever comes your way – perceived good or bad – is a blessed and humble way of seeing and living in the world. This will elevate you spiritually.

To help illustrate what I'm saying there's a very old Sufi story about a man whose son captured a strong, beautiful, wild horse, and all the neighbors told the man how fortunate he was.

The man patiently replied, 'We will see.' One day the horse threw the son, who broke his leg, and all the neighbours told the man how cursed he was that the son had ever found the horse. Again, the man answered, 'We will see.' Soon after the son broke his leg, soldiers came to the village and took away all the able-bodied young men, but the son was spared. When the man's friends told him how lucky the broken leg was, the man would only say, 'We will see.' Gratitude for participating in the mystery of life is like this.

The Sufi poet Rumi speaks of the mystery of life coming from God in his poem *The Guest House:* 'This being human is a guest house. Every morning a new arrival. A joy, a depression, a meanness, some momentary awareness comes as an unexpected visitor.

'Welcome and entertain them all! Even if they're a crowd of sorrows who violently sweep your house empty of its furniture. Still, treat each guest honorably. He may be clearing you out for some new delight.'

Gratitude practised with this level of Surrender and Trust cultivates a deep sense of joy and contentment and balances out your tendency to focus on the negative.

Count Your Blessings

There are numerous ways to use conscious awareness and present-centred mindfulness to cultivate a feeling of gratitude, even in the darkest of moments.

It's easy to acknowledge your appreciation and gratitude when things are going well for you, but it's twice as easy to forget to be grateful when you don't feel things are going well or the way you wanted them to go. But, if you could, this would be more beneficial and helpful for you in the long run, especially if you're struggling emotionally.

As part of my workshops I ask students to acknowledge and respond to a challenging situation which is currently causing them deep stress by naming it as such. I ask them to honour the difficulty, pain and struggle that's presenting, but then to also find something within the situation which they can be grateful for, something that brings depth to their understanding of who they are, or of life itself.

Often the most challenging and painful experiences in your life will bring you your greatest opportunities for spiritual and emotional growth, if only you take the time to see and process them.

When I made the decision to leave the stability of my career and rip open my persona to go in search of my True Self and start the journey of fulfilling my promise to God, needless to say it was emotionally one of the hardest, most confusing times I've faced, which led to my dark night of my soul. This confusion and my dark night put a lot of pressure on my marriage. My husband couldn't understand why I would leave a career which to him looked so rewarding, nor could he understand why I was so seemingly sad when I'd gotten everything I'd asked for: the opportunity to stay at home and write my book, one of my life long dreams. My husband is a Virgo and a carpenter and is used to being able to fix things when they are broken. He struggled to understand my sadness and struggled with his not knowing how to 'fix it'.

It was a really tough time where we both had to dig deep emotionally and spiritually to work through our lack of understanding of each other and our collective fears. I talk more about this in Part Two of the book, but for now I use this to illustrate my point because at the time it was devastating, but now, through the other side, I'm grateful for that period because we're closer than we've ever been, with more openness and oneness in our marriage than I thought possible.

At the time it took every ounce of energy I had, but I held on to the faith and belief that there's always wisdom in suffering, and there's always something to be thankful for. My husband and I were at loggerheads, but he was still an amazing father and provider of security and comfort for me and my children. I chose, through cultivating gratitude, to focus on all the wonderful things he did rather than the negative. Rather than blaming him for not understanding me or supporting me the way I felt he should, I was able to see his point of view and forgive him for not being what I wanted and needed him to be.

Take a moment now to reflect on your own attitude of gratitude. Begin by asking yourself if you believe that to be able to express gratitude you have to feel good right now? Or can you find something to be grateful about even when you're struggling in a situation that feels like there's no happy ending?

If it's the first, consider if that isn't quite small-minded and implies that your gratitude is based upon an exchange that says to the Universe, 'As long as I feel good, as long as I get what I want, I'll be grateful; if not, forget it, there's nothing to be grateful for.'

This isn't the depth of gratitude that leads to a mystical, direct experience of God and life. It's more like blackmail or an emotional demand of God. The kind of thing a young child would say, right? Give me those sweeties or I won't be grateful for everything you provide. Or, I'll be grateful when you start buying me all the toys I want. Would you accept that from your child? Hell, no. You'd be appalled at how ungrateful your child was being, considering everything you do for them, such as providing food, shelter and love, right?

Well, that's the same as saying you can't find anything to be grateful for right now and you'll just wait until you get that thing you want (or think you want) before you start being grateful to God.

That doesn't cut it, I'm afraid.

If you were to take a few minutes right now to mentally note the many people who have invisibly served you by providing medicine, shelter, safety, food, and education and kindness, and then to make a list of all the things you are grateful for, how long would that list be? Twenty items? A hundred? Five hundred?

Most likely you'd include your health, your mind's ability to function well, family, friends, and freedom. But would you include the basics, like a safe place to sleep, a comfortable warm home, clean air and water, food, and access to medicine? What about for the earth and nature itself, blue skies, a child's laughter, the smell of spring, the tang of salt, the sweetness of sugar, or that first morning cup of coffee?

I have a ritual when I get up in the morning and that's to take the time it takes to boil the kettle to enjoy the smell of my fresh coffee. For me, there's little that's yummier. It literally warms my heart in the morning and makes me feel joy to my belly. It's a small act that brings me so much pleasure and really helps me start the day in the best way possible – I start it with genuinely being grateful for the small stuff. This feeling of instant joy and warming familiarity leads to other feelings of gratitude: the silence of being awake in the morning; the capacity and space to read; the enjoyment of a really good novel, and so on.

The making of a list like the above isn't meant to make you feel indebted or guilty that you have to make a list to see all the things to be grateful for in your life, it's intended to help you see more clearly how life really is, because when those negative goggles cloud your vision it's hard to see there's always something to feel grateful for.

You can use your list as a reflective meditation to help you become aware of a deeper meaning to, and deeper experience of, your life. You can learn to take off the negative goggles which have made seeing life negatively on a daily basis a really bad habit that prevents you from feeling the miracle of your life.

When you look at how much moaning you do versus how much gratitude you feel, you realise how far off your emotional responses are from your real situation.

As with any light there is always a shadow and learning about gratitude is no exception to the rule. If you're not mindful and conscious of your Ego when cultivating a feeling of gratitude, Ego will start to use it against you. Remember that back-door trick it likes to play? Well, here's a good example. When gratitude comes from your Ego mind it manifests as a hopeless or helpless attitude, which is only disguised as gratitude, and expresses itself in a self-defeating, passive voice. For example, 'Yes, these things are wrong and unfair, but I should be grateful for what I have.' Or, 'At least we have this.' Or, 'Compared to these people, look how much better off we are.'

Gratitude is not an excuse for being or feeling passive in your life. Don't sit at home thinking, 'Well, I shouldn't strive for what I'd really love to do and achieve my dreams because I should just be grateful for what I already have.' I know that yarn because I've heard it too. You can be grateful for everything you have, and still have goals and ambitions. If that's the kind of thing going through your head, then that's your Ego, not your True Self. You're not excused from working to become a more whole person, and creating a better life for you, your loved ones and all beings.

Finding Grace Through Gratitude

The words 'gratitude' and 'grace' share a common origin, the Latin word *gratus*, meaning 'pleasing' or 'thankful'. When you are in a deep state of gratitude, you will often spontaneously feel the presence of grace, which is the presence of God.

Take a moment to reflect on this: you, with all your Ego and very human flaws, have been chosen for an opportunity to consciously taste and experience life, to know and understand it for what it is, and to make a difference in the world. This gift of a conscious life is grace itself, even when your life is filled with stress, sorrow and difficulty. It may not feel like a gift at the time but remember there's a bigger picture, always.

When the great philosopher and writer Henry Thoreau went into retreat at Walden Pond, he and his friend Ralph Emerson had been studying Hindu, Buddhist, and Taoist texts. Thoreau famously wrote: 'I went to the woods because I wished to live deliberately, to front only the essential facts of life and see if I could not learn what it had to teach, and not, when I came to die, discover that I had not lived.' He understood that living consciously, living in an awakened state, living a happy life was a gift, for which the highest form of gratitude was knowing and understanding this in all its depths.

This gift of conscious life, of having a mind that can

know 'this moment is like this' is the root of all wonder from which gratitude flows. The wonder, the mystery, is that you, like everyone else, are given this short, precious time of conscious embodiment in which you can directly know life for yourself. However you find life to be cruel or kind, sorrowful or joyful, bland or stimulating, indifferent or filled with love, you get the privilege of knowing it first-hand.

Having gratitude for the grace of conscious human embodiment evolves into the practice of selfless gratitude, in which your concerns slowly but surely shift from being mostly about yourself and those close to you to being about all living beings. As we've talked about throughout this book, this is what gives you a sense of a meaningful life and purpose. As this happens, it transforms the way you see the world and, believe it or not, you need less and less in the way of good fortune and material possessions.

It becomes enough that there are those who are happy, who are receiving love, who are safe, and who have a promising future. It's not that you wouldn't like good things for yourself, but your sense of well-being is no longer dependent, and that's the buzz word here, on things that exist outside of you. You're able to rejoice that even amidst all life's suffering there still exists real joy.

You realise that suffering, joy, light and dark are part of a mysterious whole; in fact, they're kind of the same thing. When this state of selfless gratitude starts to blossom, your mind becomes quieter and your heart receives its first taste of the sweet release from fear and wanting, and returns to Divine love. This is grace. This is what it is to be aligned and connected to God.

Positive Meditation and Journalling Exercise

Try this! If you're going through a negative funk right now, take a step back, do a small deep breathing mindfulness exercise to prepare, such as the one at the end of Chapter 5, then sit down with your journal and a pen and start to watch the thoughts that are consuming your mind in this moment.

Write them all down and get them out on to paper.

What's not working in your life? What do you want more of?

Now flip that around and focus on what's working well. Even when everything seems to be collapsing around you there's always something going well or something that you're proud of – if you're completely honest you'll see it.

Write it down and express a deep, heart-centred gratitude for it. Spend time doing this, don't rush.

Now notice how shifting your focus from the negative sense of 'I lack', to gratitude and a positive sense of 'I have', changes how you feel.

Tip: to magnify your intention to feel deeper gratitude, use this essential oil blend:

Essential Oil Recipe

Blend:

Frankincense: connects you to the Divine and to God in order to help you speak and manifest your truth.

Wild Orange: uplifting, joyful and super cheerful. It's so hard not to feel joy in your heart when smelling wild orange essential oil.

Myrhh: a sacred oil of wisdom. Myrhh connects you to your True Self and helps you express gratitude from a place of alignment and an authentic sense of Self.

Now that you've reflected a little, learned a little more about being kind to yourself and the need to make time for you, to ensure the absolute best for your family, and have been introduced to how a spiritual practice can bring healing to your mind, body and soul, the next part of the book is to apply this to your relationships with your partner and your children.

If you've been following the exercises then you should already be noticing a change in the way you interact with your partner and children, and even how you show up in the world in terms of knowing more of what you do and don't want.

This is where it all starts to come together.

PART TWO

8

Relationships Are Work

'No one is sent by accident to anyone'
– A Course in Miracles

It's one thing to make the decision to work on yourself, to create a life where you're living from a place of True Self and authenticity, but what about when it's not just you? What about when the choices you make for yourself, such as career choices, fitness, life ambition, dreams and life choices, what about when they affect those around you?

Let's face it, life is rarely just about us and how we choose to live day by day. For many women this is what stops them from even trying to put their own happiness first and make their dreams a reality. Have you ever told yourself that you just don't have time to go to that (fill in the blank) class, or take that (fill in the blank) course because your time has to be with your family, your partner or your children? Have you ever felt guilty about even considering going on that retreat to get a little 'you' time, or have you ever felt scared of the impact your new dream business venture would have on your relationship? I know I did, and I know it stopped me from really going all out in pursuing my dreams for too many years.

When I got clear and courageously honest with myself, I was afraid that I'd have to sacrifice my relationship with my husband and my children to make my dreams a reality. But actually it was the opposite that was true. The lies I'd told myself were just another way of Ego holding me back. I was afraid, and I didn't need to be.

Whether for better or for worse our relationships come to act as mirrors and teach us more about who we are and what we need to learn in order to grow and achieve our purpose in this lifetime. This is true for our passionate love relationships, our friendships, parental relations and, of course, our children.

'In every relationship, good or bad, there is an opportunity for growth for those with eyes to see.'

Falling in love, choosing a life partner and choosing to raise children together is a beautiful thing. Anyone can join a monastery and commit their lives to their spiritual growth when it's just them. But throw in love, a relationship and possibly even children, and it's a whole new playing field. With so many personalities, values, beliefs, Egos and agendas in the mix, it can often be excruciating and exhausting –and yet blissful at the same time.

When you enter into a loving and long-term relationship, you're agreeing to love this person unconditionally.

Loving relationships that enhance your spiritual growth come from a place of acceptance. Are you accepting of all your partner's values and quirky behaviours? Do you share the same ideals when raising children? Sadly, when most women enter into this kind of commitment these things are not always at the forefront of their minds. So many women seem to get caught up in the romance of it all, and too many never stop to consider if they can accept and grow with this person for the rest of their lives.

In theory it sounded good to me when I said Yes, but then, in reality, let's be honest, sometimes the rest of my life can feel like a long time!

Can you apply everything from Part One of this book to your relationships? Yes, you absolutely can, and you must, even if your partner isn't on board. It doesn't stop you from being the change. In fact, there's no better place to show up authentically, from a place of True Self than in your marriage, love relationship or relationship with your children.

Understanding and applying acceptance in your relationships is crucial for a sense of mutual respect and an all-round happy relationship. Love is at its deepest when you fully accept someone for who they are and in turn they accept you, too. This is Divine love being embodied between two people. You can use this connection between each other to raise your levels of consciousness; this is what Christ Consciousness is all about. Think Mary Magdalene and Jesus. Theirs was said to be a balanced relationship of Sun and Moon energies, yin and yang. They complemented each other and their love was an earthly celebration of Divine masculine/feminine, mother/father God energy.

There's no control in a healthy relationship; one partner doesn't seek to control, dominate or oppress the other, emotionally or physically. This isn't love. This behaviour is Ego incarnate in your relationship.

Some of the biggest challenges I see people facing in relationships are when the couple stops accepting – or hasn't ever accepted – the other for exactly who they are, and when controlling insecurities start dominating the relationship.

Taking each other for granted is a sign of mindless living, as is boredom in your relationship. When someone begins to feel 'bored' it's because they're projecting their inner 'boredom' and discontent for themselves on to their partner.

Agreeing on your common values and even how to raise your children, and not taking out your frustrations of an imperfect life on each other, are common challenges that couples face. These can turn very quickly from molehills to mountains if they're not worked at daily with conscious awareness of your Ego and the part it plays in your relationship. It's important to check in regularly with both yourself and each other to ensure communication is flowing, and that you're both on the same page. If this doesn't happen it's very easy for the relationship to break down.

Manage Your Expectations

So here I encourage you to throw out your romantic novels! Because it's my belief that many women today have an idealistic expectation of relationships and love, and it's this unrealistic expectation that ultimately sets them up to fail in finding 'Mr Perfect'. When I was a young woman – actually, right up until I met my husband at the ripe old age of 30 – my friends and I used to call our future husband, whoever he may be, 'Mr D', which was short for Mr Destiny. It sounds silly now but I, like so many other women, bought into this romantic fantasy that there was one person in the whole world for me and when I found him everything would be perfect.

Now, I'm not saying I don't believe in love, or love at first sight or there even being a soul mate. What I am saying is, when you find your Perfect Partner, and start living with them and being exposed to their daily quirks and eccentricities, and then possibly trying to raise a family together, if you're not self-aware it's very easy to end up feeling hugely disillusioned and disappointed because, guess what, they're human too, and life just isn't all about you, roses and Paris trips.

Much of someone's discontent and dismay in their relationship comes from grasping, striving or desperately pushing and wanting the relationship and the other person to be something they're just not. It's this grasping and attachment to a false dream which causes both internal and external struggle, frustrations and a feeling of being dissatisfied.

The truth is, sharing a life with someone is really hard, no matter how much 'crazy' love there is. I put an emphasis on the word crazy because sometimes that's what love can make you feel: crazy. Either crazy happy or crazy mad. Either way, that's not love, that's hormones, that's Ego, that's grasping and that's not healthy. If you're living inside your relationships, constantly wanting and needing something from them, constantly feeling unfulfilled, bored, rejected or dismayed, then chances are your expectations are too high and you're attaching your happiness to them instead of taking responsibility for it yourself. (Either that, or you are absolutely with the wrong person. But, for the purposes of this book, I'm going to assume you're with the person you really want to be with.)

If that's the case, I know you're not going to want to hear that and many of you right now are going to be screaming at me, saying, 'What?! It's not me! It's all them.' Let me guess, they don't do the dishes, or they don't take you out enough, or they just expect too much from you. The kids never call them at night when they've had a bad dream and why is it always you who needs to decide what you're having for dinner?

At least I can certainly say that's what goes on in my mind sometimes, and it's the main frustration I've heard so many other women talk about, too. When I first started living with my husband, and the honeymoon phase began to fade, I used to think it was just me. Fortunately, I'm an inquisitive, often nosey, person who has no problem being open about the challenges of everyday married life. So, I'd ask women friends questions about things such as who did the cleaning, or the cooking, or even emptying the bins. The answers were all the same. I'd tune into other women's conversations in places like coffee shops to hear what their frustrations and challenges were compared to my own, and again the complaints were all the same. Of course, this was actually a great relief to me as for a moment there I really thought I'd been served a dud. But no, it turns out I, too, am human and often live from my Ego, only thinking of things from my own perspective: my feelings, my pain, my suffering. It's only when you learn to check in and try to see things from your partner's point of view that you realise there are always two sides to every story and they're probably either completely unaware of your internal fury, or are feeling the same way about something you've done/ not done.

Relationships – all relationships – need work. Constantly. And when you add raising children into the mix, it goes beyond work. If you're going to learn how to help your relationship grow, and be happy, then this is a fact you're going to have to accept right now.

Another fact you're going to have to accept is that it's so easy for you to believe you're the only one putting the work in, and for you to often feel taken for granted. But going down that road can often be hugely destructive and difficult to come back from. It's true, relationships are a journey of ups and downs and highs and lows. However, what isn't so well known or well accepted is that mostly these highs and lows come from you. Remember how your Ego projects out into the world on all those around you? Remember how what you feel inside, sometimes even what you're not consciously aware of, you put out into the world? When you're living with someone and sharing responsibilities with them, you can't hold back many of your demons. They will, and they do, project from you on to the closest people that come into your space.

Now that you understand from Part One the principles and practice of self-awareness, acceptance (of yourself and others), trust, surrender and compassion (for yourself and others), you can build on that and learn on a deeper level about your relationship with your partner and how you can move through your own projections, accept what your issues are, and support your partner in moving through theirs, embodying that Divine love from heaven on earth. Remember, nobody can make you feel something you don't already feel about yourself in some way; everything is a projection. Those closest to you are your clearest mirrors and if you embrace this, it's a wonderful opportunity for growth.

To start, it's crucially important you learn that you're not always right. I'm going to say that again: you're not always right! Sometimes you're wrong, and you just can't see the other person's perspective because you're so incensed, you believe so hard that you've been wronged, they take you for granted, how dare they... but it's not always the case. And you can bet your bottom dollar, if you're feeling something, the other person is feeling it too. So, for example, if you're feeling taken for granted, that's an energy that exists between both of you. Your partner could be feeling exactly the same thing, which is leading them to behave in a way that makes you feel that way, too.

This is where your reflective journal really comes into play. If you have awareness of your inner fears and insecurities, you can act on them before they start influencing your behaviour and actions towards your partner.

You can't change the other person in your relationship – don't ever believe that's possible, because it's not. If one person in the relationship is dominating the other and trying to force change on them, it simply won't work. No one should have to change for someone else. If change is to happen, it must come from them as an individual (with your support and love, of course) but never because it's something you want from them or are forcing on them in some way.

Communicating with Awareness

For this reason, learning to communicate in a heart-centred way in your relationship is obviously critical. I'm sure you know this. But I use the word 'learning' for a reason. Often when people talk about communicating openly, they think ok, I'm just going to own my feelings and talk about them. They forget that when you talk, you have to learn to listen, too. This is often the biggest skill you'll have to learn. It's not just listening with your ears, it's hearing with your heart that is the secret to effective communication. So many lose the ability to really hear and feel what the other person is saying and feeling when they become so distracted and busy with their own lives. Couples forget to speak to each other, let alone how to speak to each other, or even to pause to hear each other.

Through the art of presence and stillness, you can tune into what your issues are, own them and hear how your partner is feeling, too. When you're able to do this, your communication comes from the heart, its foundation is compassion and love, not an attack or an Ego game of blame, where the person communicating how they feel is just accusing and attacking in the disguise of 'talking about it'. For example, 'This is how I feel because…' is better than, 'This is how you made me feel', because no one can make you feel anything. You are, after all, the master of your feelings. Putting blame on to someone else is accusatory and really just asking for conflict. It also prevents you from taking responsibility for yourself, and that is never good in general, but especially in your relationship. It's so important that you own your own feelings, actions and behaviours for your relationship's growth as well as for your own personal growth.

When issues arise it's so easy to get caught up in the intensity of your emotions and start arguing for your rights and point of view and then forget about the other person's. Arguing and disagreements are natural and common but, in extreme cases, things can also get dark and personal with blame and accusations being thrown around, which, if you could have stayed present and aware of your triggers, wouldn't necessarily have occurred. If you can remain present and connected to your True Self during these times of intense communication, so that your Ego isn't doing all of the talking, navigating your way through these challenging and often highly emotional times can be far smoother and far less painful for everyone involved.

Bringing full awareness to your communication is really helpful when you're both caught up in your respective Egos and your emotions are leading from the front. When you're highly emotional it's virtually impossible to see the other person's side, but remember – there are always two sides. When you've triggered your Ego, it is speaking for you, so it's really important to try and become present in your body and connected to your True Self so that you become fully aware and conscious. You become the watcher and not the thinker.

Mindful listening is a great and effective way to give your partner your full, undistracted attention, letting them know you see them and you hear them.

Remembering all the principles and techniques you learned in Part One of this book, follow the exercise below to deepen your communication and connection with your partner.

Mindful Listening Exercise

Remember that you can be, and can lead, the change you want to see in your relationship. Take a few moments alone before going to your partner to talk so you can ground and connect with yourself.

Surrender to your Inner Teacher and let Divine love work through you here for the good of all involved. Prepare yourself by connecting with a few deep breaths to attune to your True Self so you can recognise what is real for you and what is your Ego talking. Remind yourself at this point that your partner has a point of view as well. Start cultivating that feeling of connectedness by channelling compassion for them and towards them. Use the Tonglen exercise for compassion in Chapter 4 to do this, it's really powerful. What are your partner's basic values? Remind yourself this person is a good person with good values. They're not the enemy (hopefully).

Ask yourself honestly what's this resistance and conflict really about? Have the courage to hear the truth in the answer that comes to you. It takes courage and a spine of steel to be honest and admit to your insecurities and inner demons but remember, you're a stronger, wiser person for it. True strength and emotional intelligence is always truthful.

What is standing in the way of you talking openly and calmly? Remember, you're human, too; you have triggers. What triggers could be being activated for you right now that your having awareness of could help you see the other person's point of view more clearly?

As you come together to talk, allow your conversation to flow as it normally would and allow your grounded self to anchor you in this moment, so you become attuned and fully present. Begin by noticing the mood and body language of your partner. Are they talking quickly or slowly? Does your partner appear open and engaged in this conversation, or are they more withdrawn or perhaps quieter than usual and more reflective? Giving your full, grounded and present attention helps you to maintain your calm and adapt to the conversation as it unfolds. So, rather than getting caught up in heated, frustrated emotions you can remain centred, calm and aware of your triggers, and theirs, which may be being pushed in the intensity of the moment.

Make sure that as you talk to each other you pause every now and then, just briefly, to form your response to your partner's shared thoughts and feelings. This allows you to think about your response and choice of words rather than talking reactively from your Ego.

Jackie's Story

As Jackie sat across from me on her kitchen stool, she was nervously watching me take my coat off and settle into my chair. I could see she wasn't sure what to say or do next.

'I've never done this before – asked for help, that is,' was her first comment.

Jackie had contacted me asking for an appointment because her marriage had crumbled after eight good (to her mind) solid years. Jackie said that she had absolutely no idea about her husband's unhappiness or infidelity and was now left completely heartbroken, with no idea how to pick herself back up for her children. Jackie was hoping I could help her make sense of the end of her marriage and of how she could ever move forward.

As we talked, it became clear to me that things had started to take a sour turn when their children arrived. Intimacy had stopped, as had all open and honest communication as a partnership. Both had been existing in a marriage of friendship at best. 'When my first baby was born things were still ok, it was only when my second was born that I really struggled as I was feeling exhausted. Throughout the years that passed I stopped caring about his feelings because I was too consumed by my own feelings of discontent. It felt like I was doing everything alone and I resented him for it. But I did nothing to change my situation and instead martyred on. So, we stopped making time for each other and stopped having sex. Everything else just seemed more important.'

It seemed her husband had also really struggled with this change in Jackie and in their relationship, but because of the breakdown in communication, wasn't able to communicate his feelings. Instead, he appeared to shut down, said he didn't recognise her any more, and found her and their life together boring. Jackie was left crushed as her husband left her for another woman and their marriage ended.

'I just got lost in the everyday business of family and

work – it never occurred to me that my relationship would need help to grow, I thought it would grow by itself.'

I've used Jackie's story here because honestly, I could be telling the same story for so many women I've worked with or known personally. One of the most common reasons for a breakdown in a relationship is because one or both parties start taking the other for granted, and they stop making the effort to 'be' together. They start living mindlessly, without conscious intention or awareness, dreamily sleepwalking through life and only thinking about me, myself and I.

When talking about what could have been different and what could have saved her marriage, Jackie was able to see that by simply making time for herself and also making time for her and her husband to grow their relationship, their story could have been different. This brutal honesty from Jackie was inspiring. It takes courage to be this honest with yourself. Sometimes the courage is born from the darkest times of your life, but the strength and depth of the lessons learned from such courage and honesty are truly inspiring and are powerful to share with others.

One of the many reasons relationships crumble is because of the pressure of expectation that's put on them when children come along. If you can exercise the art of balance, awareness, acceptance and surrender in your relationship then you have a chance for that fairytale 'happy ever after'. However, if you coast along in the relationship with your mind distracted, always projecting out of yourself your inner insecurities and angst, always blaming the other person for your dissatisfaction in your life, or feeling the resentment linked to petty arguments, this can build into a deep bitterness and can fester into an emotionally toxic relationship. Soon this toxicity overtakes everything, breaking down your communication and understanding of one another and, of course, your intimacy together.

You must know yourself before you can healthily enter into a relationship with another person. Knowing who you are, being connected to that person and ok with them, warts and all, will stop you from blaming your partner for how you feel about yourself. It will help you recognise the difference between your insecurity and Ego triggers, and what's real and needs to be addressed. The majority of the time you'll find it's your Ego mind triggering and causing trouble where trouble doesn't need to exist. This is true for every single person on the planet. Those naïve enough to believe they're 'perfect' and don't bring any challenges or hang-ups into the relationship, are in denial. As a consequence, they will inevitably end up pushing the other person away or driving themselves away, throwing away the opportunity to have a loving partnership.

Here's a little brutal honesty from me right here, right now. And as I write this I guess I'm also projecting… Simply know this: each and every one of you reading this has flaws and quirks and are not an easy person to live with. Accept it, learn what your flaws are, then learn how to own them, let them help you grow as a woman and as a person and let go of needing to blame others for them. In short, learn how to take full responsibility for your thoughts, feelings and, most of all, actions in your relationship, because, as the old fabulous saying goes: 'It takes two to tango.'

And if you're single and reading this and you're wondering why, take a look back through your relationships, look at the patterns, and at your contribution to the breakdown.

Are you attracting the wrong person? If so, what in you is attracting them? Why? Remember, like attracts like. Is there something you fear about yourself that makes you attract that into your life in a partner and relationship? Have the courage to be open and brutally honest. Old patterns and self-sabotaging behaviours can't be changed if you refuse to see them for what they are.

And just as a footnote, ladies, please don't beat yourself up about this… we are all human, we're all flawed and we're all here to learn. Don't let Ego find another way to torture you and beat you up!

9

Intimacy and Sex

'The body can become a vehicle to that which is beyond body, and sex energy can become a spiritual force' – Osho

Relationships aren't just about getting through the day-to-day humdrum of life. They can also provide an opportunity for deep spiritual growth, not only from an emotional level, as we've looked at, but with mind and body as well. To deepen your relationship and connection to each other, intimacy and your sex life are really important.

Our sexual health is vitally important to our overall wellbeing – physically, emotionally, mentally, socially and spiritually. It's woven into the story of where we've come from, where we are now and where we're going.

Sex can be so much more than just a physical body experience, either alone or with another as you tune into yourself or your partner emotionally and take the time to enjoy the experience and come into the present moment. No pun intended.

It really is an essential practice of soulful and relationship 'self-care' and should be as prioritised in your lives as taking your vitamins, eating a healthy diet and taking the bins out on bin day.

Our sexual energy is our life force – it's the pulse of Kundalini Divine love energy flowing through our bodies throughout our lives. It supports your health, creativity and a long life. Ever noticed that youthful glow after an orgasm?

Unfortunately, for many sex and intimacy are the first things to slide when life gets busy. Or, worse still, something they've never been able to connect to or feel comfortable with because of historic toxic projections they've experienced from their culture or other adults around them.

Also, for many women there can be a struggle with body confidence, especially with today's pressures on women, and then you have children… It's pretty hard to see your body as sexy after that.

Many women report no longer feeling sexy or desired by their partners and view the changes which have happened to their bodies from carrying and giving birth to children with embarrassment and, sadly, even shame.

Not to mention that taking care of children, running a home and having a day job can be truly exhausting, especially when you live on auto-pilot and survival mode all the time. It's very hard, even impossible, for a woman to ever feel relaxed enough or tuned into her body enough to experience desire when she is exhausted. And that's a huge problem for a woman, because desire for a woman is emotional. Even though you feel it through your body, you need to get out of your head and pause for long enough to experience any sexual urges you may have. And, believe it or not, it's at times when you feel least sexy, when you're at your most stressed, that sex should be prioritised to get that vital energy force moving through the body, waking it up a little, and reconnecting you to your creative True Self.

Just like meditation, exercise and anything else that you know is good for you, sex and orgasm should be a priority in your life. I know when I'm feeling really inspired and creative and connected to the Divine, because I feel sexually aroused. For me, they go hand in hand. If my sex life is off, or I lose interest in sexual desire, it's a sign that I've slipped away from my connection to God and Divine love and, as a result, my creative life force and energy are blocked.

Stress Buster

Sex and intimacy are deeply relaxing and energising at the same time. Your body releases lots of fabulous feel-good endorphins which are known to fight stress, build immunity and produce more collagen in the body, so you not only feel happier on the inside, you'll have that sexy youthful glow, too. It also produces oxytocin, which is known as the 'love hormone' and is responsible for deepening relationships. When you're feeling run ragged, stressed, exhausted and, as a result, are struggling with your self-esteem and confidence (and it happens to us all), this is the very time you need your partner's love and affection the most, or you need to spend some time with yourself. Sexual desire, masturbation and loving, trusting intimacy with yourself or another is not wrong and is not dirty. If you have any hang-ups here or are triggering and emotionally reacting to this chapter, then take some time and go to your journal now to reflect on why. Most issues come from negative past experiences, which may have been painful and left emotional scarring, or from feeling repressed and insecure about your own body and sexual identity. Whatever may be happening for you, remember self-compassion and don't beat yourself up. Your past experiences don't have to define who you are and how you see things now. Remember, you are absolutely worthy of loving yourself.

However, if you are in a relationship, intimacy between you and your partner is so important for so many reasons: it brings you back together and keeps that bond sealed; it fosters an intimate, open and honest, trusting relationship where it's easy to communicate freely with one another; and it helps you recharge when stressed. There's nothing like feeling loved and wanted to make a woman feel sexy and confident when she needs it most. On the other hand, if intimacy isn't happening on a regular basis, feelings of frustration and a sense of 'me, myself and I' can take hold, which can push you further away from your partner and thus increase that further sense of isolation and shut down. And, as we've previously looked at throughout the book, when you start living from a place of isolation it's you living from your Ego. This can cause thoughts, feelings and, in turn, actions or behaviours that are not from a place of love and compassion, and are not in your best interests, nor in the interests of others around you. For example, if your heart isn't being fed, if you don't feel that you're loved and wanted, it's easy to try and find love and acceptance in other areas or even with other people. For some, having a distraction such as food or alcohol, which brings a temporary and quick fix of comfort, can fill the void, as can busying yourself in gossip or social media. But these are all temporary measures, again driven by your Ego, and come from a place of insecurity. A bit like burying your head in the sand.

If you've never felt connected to or confident in your own body, or if you no longer feel sexy and confident about your body since having children, then letting go of fears and hang-ups about sex and your body is not only crucial to your relationship but also to your self-esteem, overall confidence and ultimate happiness.

But how can you 'let go' of such deeply personal insecurities about your body? I believe the answer to that is, again, for you to look at your Ego triggers. We know the pressure these days for a woman to have a certain body type and look a certain way is everywhere. But I believe that pressure has been there for a long time; it's not new. Like fashion, it's something that's ever changing, so why is it causing so much pressure today? For example, belly dancers were preferred to be rounder in the hips and stomachs in Egyptian times. Nowadays, a woman having a six-pack is considered sexy, and it's the same for men. There are periods in history where it was fashionable for men, usually in the upper classes, to look more feminine – a gentleman would not have had bulging muscles from working hard in the fields. Shapes of bodies have changed over the years, as fashion dictates. It has always been like this.

So why now is it affecting our self-esteem to the extent where it's making people sick? Although I've already mentioned what I think of media images and society's expectations about what's hot and what's not, I don't believe it's all down to them.

Live with Passion and Purpose

Self-esteem, confidence, and simply feeling good about yourself and your body comes from within you. You could have great abs, and legs up to your arm pits, but if you're not happy within yourself, if you're not connected to your True Self and living an authentic life with passion and purpose, you'll always look at yourself from the insecure eyes of the Ego mind. Confidence in all areas comes from knowing and liking who you are; and as sex, for women in particular, is such an energetic emotional thing, knowing and liking who you are is fundamental, crucial even.

Seeing yourself as sensual and sexy starts with liking who you are first. Liking who you are starts with actually knowing who you are. Just as we've learned in the first part of this book.

So, before your partner can see you as a sensual sexual being, you need to see yourself this way – and, what's more, you need to like what you see. If you have lost your connection with feeling sensual and feminine (or perhaps have never felt this way) then only you have the power to do the work to change that.

Just as a footnote: be aware that since desire and sex are such emotional topics and issues for so many, it can cause people around you to project their insecurities on to you. Even our close friends do this. If you are strong and secure in yourself and your sexuality, this can and does cause insecure projections to be aimed at you, like jealousy, spite and anger. It's a sad and maddening shame but if you've experienced this from another woman, just let it go and remind yourself of who you are. It's a sad truth that we women can often be the cruellest towards our own gender. When it comes to love and sex, insecurity can be a loaded gun of truly venomous spite.

Send that person or those people love and compassion (take some for yourself first) because it's their inner pain and torment that's doing the talking and that's what's saddest of all. Don't ever apologise for being you and for being confident and happy.

Now, if knowing that sexual energy can be so transforming and good for you isn't enough to get you prioritising and scheduling the time for it, think about this: it's also crucial as a way of connecting to yourself to own your sexual feminine energy. The sexual and sensual energy that surges through your body is part of who you are. In yoga we call it the Kundalini, and in Buddhism the Tantra awakening. Raising the Kundalini energy is a practice to bring you closer to the Divine and to explore your sexual energy. When this energy is in balance it feeds you with joy and contentment but, when out of balance or repressed, you're once again disconnected from your True Self and from the Divine energy which connects us all. Every woman should allow herself to tune into and experience her sexual nature and the energy of the Kundalini, to experience fully her 'sexy' self and connect deeper to her True Self and the Universe.

Just because you've became a mother, doesn't mean your sexual needs die and this energy within you no longer exists. In fact, as a woman who has carried and borne a child, this energy is never more present in your body. Your connection to the Universe is more powerful and vital. Closing off or losing this part of themselves has been a huge problem for many of the women I've worked with. They report not feeling sexy any more and seeing themselves only through the eyes of their children. They see themselves only as a mother, which can be destructive because as a woman you're so much more. You must pause for long enough to go inside yourself and connect to that. Just because you've had children, the other aspects of you aren't dead. They're very much alive and to ignore them or repress them brings imbalance to the mind, body and spirit, which ultimately equals unhappiness and ill health.

Many women feel that they weren't actually a sexual person before children. There are many reasons for this (enough for a whole other book) but, if this was you, then now is your chance to discover that side of yourself. Motherhood, if you let it, can bring out the best in you and, with a loving relationship, together you can use your intimate life to blend mind, body and spirit to new depths of self-growth and joy. Now really is the time to discover your True Self on every level.

To start connecting with your sensual self you need to start first with setting the intention to love and accept your body and your sexual nature. Remember, your body is miraculous and beautiful – try to let go of any judgement and self-criticism.

Make time for you and your partner to practise what you've learned from previous chapters about being in the moment, surrendering to all that the moment has and letting go of your 'to do' list. There's a full exercise at the end of this chapter to help you practise this together.

First, here's an exercise to help you reconnect with your

sensual self, which in turn will help you reconnect to your body and grow in confidence:

Sensual Exercise

Come to a seated position in front of a mirror and begin by taking three deep breaths, letting go of tension and stress on the exhalation.

Place your hands on your womb or belly and begin to feel connected to your body, feeling your breath as it expands, lifting your whole belly. As you exhale, make the effort to consciously draw your belly inwards towards your spine.

Repeat this as you allow your mind to settle and come into a present-centred awareness. Let go of fears and judgement around how your body looks and feels.

Gaze at yourself in the mirror and focus your intention on feeling your breath rise and fall in your belly.

Repeat the following statements:

I am beautiful, and I am worthy of love.
My body is smoking hot, strong and healthy.
I am worthy of love and sexual pleasure.
I feel good about my sexuality and all that I desire.
I have the right to express my desires to my partner in perfect trust and love.

I have the Divine right to feel confident in who I am and to harness my feminine Goddess energy for everyone to see and feel in my presence.

If you're in a relationship it's important to prioritise time for intimacy for both of you. Remember, as busy people, if you don't schedule it, it doesn't happen.

Get away from distractions: no television, no phones.

I think having a regular date night is crucial as a couple and, if you can't get out, then just stay in. You can do things like cook together, have a bath together, sit and talk without distractions and, of course, find time to do the exercise that follows.

Tantra Based Exercise (1)

Make sure you will not be interrupted and that this time is only for you and your partner. Make time and space available that feels safe, and where you won't be disturbed.

Begin to concentrate fully on each other. Taking all that you've learned from surrendering and being in the present moment from Part One, let go of any thoughts and worries that may be coming to your mind. Remember to remain present and aware.

If your mind feels distracted, return to the moment by using your sensory experience to ground you into your body. Remember that you're using this time to reconnect and come back together after living in haste and often being separated because of the chores of daily life. So, no talking of anything other than being together and what you both want and like.

Take the pressure off reaching orgasm this time. Clear your minds and surrender to everything that feels good in this particular moment.

Sometimes music is good, toys or lubrication. Don't be afraid to experiment and explore. If you want to really connect with each other spiritually, try this next exercise to cultivate a conscious and present sensuality. It will enliven and deepen your connection to each other and your spiritual and relationship growth.

Tantra Based Exercise (2)

It's useful to set a timer here for each of you to massage the other for about ten minutes or more. Whilst being massaged bring your awareness to feeling your body in the present moment. Enjoy each touch sensually and individually. Your intention is to be fully present; the timer will help you relax into the moment. When it's your turn, do the same when giving as you would when receiving. Massage is a great way to soothe and relax each other into forgetting about the worries and stresses of the day.

Now bring this same present-centred awareness to sitting in front of each other and kissing. Enjoy each moment of the kiss. You should intentionally feel and experience the kiss instead of being distracted elsewhere. Don't worry if you do get distracted by the chitter chatter of 'what if the kids walk in?' Or 'did I turn the dish washer on?' Remember what you learned in Part One and how to focus your mind on experiencing the present moment using your senses. You can get creative here and use this same sensory awareness to really take the time and enjoy exploring each other again in a sensual way. Feel the experience and intentionally enjoy the moment.

10

Parenting With Self Awareness

'A conscious parent is not one who seeks to
fix, or create, the "perfect" child.
This is not about perfection. A conscious parent understands
that this child has been called forth to "raise the parent" itself'
– Dr Shefali Tsabary

Before meeting my husband and having our children I was footloose and fancy free. I had a career which supported my travels and hobbies and I made the best of it. I worked as a therapist with children and families in mental health services, and I thought I knew everything there was to know about being a parent and raising children. Dare I say it, I was even a little judgemental. I knew all there was to know from a theory perspective, but I had no idea how having your own child could emotionally blind you. I had yet to experience life with no sleep, or the primal call of your baby's cry, like nails being dragged down a chalk board. That cry really is designed to push every button in your body into reaction, as is their smile, their fingers, their toes and the way they gaze up at you when first born, blind like little moles. All these things are designed to keep you from abandoning them when things get tough, but all these things can also drive you to despair and push your Ego triggers to a whole new level of fear.

In the first part of the book you learned how to connect with your True Self, to recognise your projections and triggers of Ego and to understand your own suffering and learn how to manage this without reacting, practising mindfulness mediation and present-centred meditation so you become responsive, present, self-aware and compassionate.

Becoming a mother is beautiful but it can also feel like you've lost any connection to who you are

When you have children, staying connected to who you truly are can often feel impossible as your Ego is triggered. The person you once thought you were seems to disappear, and finding time for practising self-awareness and self-care – or just making time for yourself – feels impossible. For many it never gets prioritised, which leaves you at greater risk of being consumed by the role of mother you've conjured up in your Ego mind. I regularly get asked questions such as, 'How can I possibly make time for meditation, prayer or self-reflection?' These are often followed with the exclamation, 'I can't even make time to take a shower!'

I completely understand that life does get much busier and far more sleep deprived than it ever was before children, but that's not to say you can't practise your awareness or deepen your connection to yourself – it means you should make it even more of a priority.

In fact, as I mentioned, this is your time and your unique opportunity to deepen your spiritual growth. When you learn how to multi task in a modern spiritual-mum way, you'll start to see more time appear in your life. It goes back to that sense of balance and the benefits of training your mind to be focussed and present in the moment that you learned in the first part of the book. Getting out of the entanglement of haste and your emotionally over-involved mindset will help you step back, breathe and have more time in your day-to-day life. You can even step out of your busy mind by learning to combine your mindfulness practice with your daily chores, such as preparing and sitting down to the family dinner, bathing the baby, doing the house cleaning and making time to be present with your partner and children through regular family activities.

Life B.C. (Before Children)

You know once you've had a baby that you're no longer the same woman, but it's hard to see amongst the nappies and piles of laundry who you are once you become a mother. Everything changes, not just in your outer world and sleep patterns, but in your heart as you begin to experience what it's like to have an ancient sense of purpose and meaning to your life. I can't express enough how this change that takes place within you is a wonderful opportunity for self-growth and spiritual development, if you learn how to use it for exactly that.

If not, it can become a bit of a black hole that sucks you into despair and darkness and, instead of feeling you have purpose, you feel as if you are somehow lacking in your life, like something just isn't right but you can't quite put your finger on it.

It's all well and good laughing on social media about how you've had to neck two bottles of wine because your toddler had a breakdown at the store, or your teen has slammed the door in your face yet again because you dared to ask them how their day went, but this level of emotional intensity that is the joy and despair of daily motherhood can be so overwhelming and exhausting, it's really not comical any more. For some, the emotional challenges of being a modern-day mother are real, and for many the level of stress and anxiety is making them ill.

Throughout my work in mental health services and in my own experiences as a mother, I've found that it's in learning to find presence, surrendering and tuning into your True Self, practising self-compassion and present-centred awareness in every moment of what's unfolding inside and outside of yourself, which will help you manage those often highly intense and emotionally volatile parental challenges with a feeling of calmness and an air of 'I got this'.

The practices throughout this book will help you make sense of your day-to-day challenges and, especially for those of you on the journey of motherhood, you can use them to help you gain the courage and clarity to bring your dreams to life and live with meaning and purpose.

Through your awareness of yourself and your own projections you can learn to attune to the emotional states and needs of those around you and, in particular, to your children. The age of distraction, of looking outside of yourself for the answers or for temporary happiness, has massively affected how people in our society parent their children. It's so easy to let the television be the third parent in the home. Trust me, I know – I'm guilty of that too. Or that your toddler has to literally hit you across the head with their book because you're so engrossed and distracted by your friend's latest Facebook post about what a fabulous life she's leading that you haven't heard your child repeatedly asking you for a story for the last five minutes. Hands up, true story for me, too.

Have you ever noticed that the times when you find yourself shouting and snapping at your kids are usually when you've been trying to do ten things at once, and your mind is distracted? So, what happens? Frustration and a feeling of over-whelm kick in and you snap. It happens to me when I'm trying to do too much and not really doing anything well at all. That's when it's time to pull back, pause and take focussed action, dealing with one thing at a time. This example can be one moment, or one situation – or it can be how you're living life as a whole.

And it's not just your babies and small children that need your emotional attunement to them. Young adults need your present-centred emotional engagement with them and their needs just as much. They may not need it as often, but it's still very much needed.

Remembering that your children are your biggest triggers is essential when parenting because often you'll project your Ego fears and desires on to them as they grow and start to shine in their personality. Have you ever uttered the words 'she takes after me' or 'I think he's going to be just like me'? When you watch your children play or have a tantrum do you see yourself in them, very much like a mirror? And have you noticed that all the good bits come from you and all the bits which drive you mad must be your partner's or the father's side? Well, going back to what you learned about projection in the first part of the book, it's highly likely that what you see in your child that you dislike the most, that really drives you crazy, is actually that part in yourself that you don't want to own or admit to. It's your shadow staring right back at you and probably giving you a little wink, just to raise that fury some more.

If you become practised in the art of self-awareness when raising your children, you will help them to grow into themselves and blossom with confidence and an understanding that they know exactly who they are, separate from you, your expectations and the expectations of society around them. Because of this confidence and clarity, they will find a clear path to follow, making their lives their own. And, as you learn to let go of your Ego attachment, you'll be far less stressed. When you surrender to knowing that your children really are their own people, and look at them with accepting eyes and a loving heart, you can parent and guide them with more confidence and joy in an often uncertain world.

Your job as a mother, and as a parent, is to love unconditionally, to accept and to guide. It's not to try and live their lives for them nor to get them to live the life you dreamed of but for whatever reason didn't quite manage. They're not little mini versions of you, and they're not responsible for you feeling good about yourself. That burden is too heavy for anyone else to carry and yet we do often put this on to our children without even realising it.

Nowadays there seems to be an ever-increasing rise in children being compared to each other and pushed harder to be faster, smarter and more confident than the other. I swear that there is even a competition with some mothers as to how many after-school clubs and activities one's children can attend in a week or even in a day! This middle-class competitive culture seems to have sprung up out of a need to feel – and prove to society – that you're the best mother in the school playground. Everyone seems to want to outdo each other. Using their children as pawns in a game of Ego chess, these mothers are driven by fear and insecurity of not feeling or being 'good enough'. Even I am guilty of this sometimes. Remember that your Ego triggers have a way of sneaking up on you, no one living on this earth is immune. If they tell you they are, that's just their Ego talking. This is why it's so important to practise incorporating self-awareness through mindfulness and self-compassion, to know what your Ego's influence is and what's actually best for you and your child when parenting.

A time where I had to face up to one of my many Ego-driven indiscretions was when my husband and I were teaching our children to mountain bike. It's one of our favourite hobbies that we do together so it's natural to want my children to take to the sport and become pros! Being blessed with two little boys who also love riding their bikes, I found myself one day pushing my eldest to go faster and harder on a trail, encouraging him to be the best, to learn to grow and to one day be a champion mountain biking pro like all those fabulous athletes we follow and watch race on Red Bull TV. I had failed to see that my son just wasn't interested and was actually getting frustrated and resentful towards me and the whole family because of this. All my son wanted to do was get off his bike and chase the butterfly that fluttered past him, but I couldn't see that because I was too busy dreaming about and planning his future whilst getting cross and frustrated because he didn't seem interested. As a result, I started to sulk and become reactive, moody even.

Well, he did what he wanted – he got off his bike. That's when I saw him in the moment giggling with delight at chasing a beautiful butterfly (which I swear was playing with him). For me it was like taking a bullet as it suddenly hit me that I was pushing him for my own Ego needs, and not because he wanted it. He just wanted to play, and that play involved being so present in the moment that he naturally hopped off his bike and engaged in the most beautiful and innocent play that I think I have ever seen. I honestly believe that moment was the Divine right there telling me to back off, get out of my Ego, and let my son play.

That wasn't the first time my Ego was driving my thinking and my behaviour with my children, and I dare say it won't be the last. All I can do is try to stay aware of it, knowing that it's not the woman I am and not the mother I want to be, and then setting the intention to work on myself some more to bring more self-awareness to my Ego and not repeat my mistakes. If I do, I also need to remember to forgive myself for it with loving kindness and self-compassion because I'm human, and we all make mistakes. An apology in the right direction is always quite helpful too.

Being a mother isn't about being perfect, it's about loving yourself and your children enough to take responsibility for knowing that you're not. It's about fully understanding that, even though you're a mother, you don't have all the answers, and you don't get it right all the time. That's actually the beauty of motherhood and sharing your life with your family, you get the opportunity to learn and to grow together. Letting go of attachment, judgement and the demand for perfectionism from yourself frees up your children to be the perfect little imperfect people they are born to be. Being present with your children and living with awareness not only frees them from the burden of your Ego's insecurities, fears and lost dreams, it also helps you attune to their needs, helping them feel understood, accepted and appreciated.

This is, after all, all that anyone really wants. To be loved and accepted for exactly who they are. Practise this in your parenting, and the rest will unfold in its own time.

Make time in your life to be with your children and allow your children to just be present, saying 'I see you, I hear you, I'm here for you on every level'. Being still, putting the phone down, turning the television off and consciously choosing, with intention, to be present, just like you learned to do in the first part of the book, is an ideal way to connect with, and deepen your relationship to, your children and the family as a whole.

Quality Versus Quantity

Time spent this way is quality time and present, conscious quality time with your child, no matter how brief it may be, is worth so much more than oodles of time where you're distracted and in your head. When that happens, you're physically present but you're not really there, you're not emotionally available. There's a huge difference here and the difference is crucial to your children feeling loved, wanted, accepted, seen and heard.

It may please you to know that in this busy, distracted time we live in, it's really not the amount of time you spend with your children that's vital, it's the quality of undistracted time which is key to emotionally attuning to your child. That's the real game changer. It's inevitable that sometimes as a mum you have to work, sometimes for long hours. Some mums, and let's not forget dads here, even have to travel with work. You're not going to escape from that in this day and age and my belief is why should you?

We've already spoken in Chapter 3 about the importance of making time for yourself when you have children, whether that be in your career, passion or hobby. It's important that you have space and time to be you. Being with your children 24/7 is not always necessary and is not always helpful. In some cases I've worked with families where there's a mum at home all day with her child but the relationship and emotional attunement – the connection and bond – are not as secure and strong as it has been for the mum who works long hours and the child is at day care for most of the day. The reason for this is because the little free time the mum who works long hours has is spent consciously and undistractedly with her child. She's focussed and present in their time together and therefore attuned emotionally and genuinely interested in being with her child. Sadly, the mum at home who has all day to be with her child is often distracted by the TV, her phone, gossip and the boredom and disillusionment of motherhood. As she often feels isolated, she finds comfort in distractions, which temporarily make her feel good, but don't last for long. As a result, the child is often in these cases emotionally neglected, never feels heard or understood and comes to feel a nuisance as it's hushed and passed off whenever it 'bothers' its mother for some much-needed emotional attention. In such cases, the child is left feeling unaccepted and unloved.

My comparison of the two scenarios above is not to judge but to illustrate where distraction is responsible for taking one's attention away from the present moment and to show that it's not always hardship or lack of time that's causing dissatisfaction or stress in your life today. It's how you spend that time. Raising your children today isn't harder, it's just easier to be distracted – from them and from yourself. This may seem an extreme example, but I ask you to look at your day-to-day life: what do you spend your time doing? Are you distracted by work, friends, social media, making the dinner, doing the laundry or other mundane household chores?

Are you prioritising time to come together with your children and family just to 'be' together, enjoy each other's company? And in these times when you are together, are you focussed? Is the TV on in the background? Are you all sitting there on your phones talking to other people or looking at the internet? I know without conscious thought this scenario easily happens in my home. It's so easy for these distractions to creep up on us in our day-to-day lives. Using the kind of routine practice you've developed throughout this book for your own 'me time' will help you stay present and on top of such silent, yet very destructive, day-to-day behavioural patterns.

This is why planning conscious, intentional time together, where you all leave distractions behind, should be prioritised. Just as your job is, just as brushing your teeth is, and your time for yourself is, and your date night with your partner – it's all important. It's a plan, a moment in time where you plan to be present and conscious with each of your children, attuned to each other's emotional needs, with no agenda other than to enjoy each other's company in full acceptance of each other and the gift of this present moment.

Don't Just Take My Word For It

Evidence shows us that this attuned time together improves communication, depth of relationship and bonding. It also improves levels of confidence, self-esteem and resilience within the child as they grow with a feeling of being accepted, appreciated and, above all else, loved. This way of being with your child plants the seeds for them to have a secure and grounded relationship with themselves and with the world as they grow and start to spread their wings. It's a gift that only parents can give, and it's worth making the time for if you want your child to have the best opportunity to have a happy, healthy life.

The scientific community has proven that cortisol, the stress hormone responsible for depression, is not only a risk for the mother but also for children, from the baby in the womb to the angst-ridden confused teen. It's been scientifically proven both psychologically and neurologically that consistent love, affection and emotional attunement literally shape the baby's brain in the first five years of its life. But now science is also proving, through the work of renowned neuroscientist-clinician, Allan N Schore

Ph.D, that if for some reason things didn't go as planned in someone's early years, the neural pathways can also change later on in a person's life, through the engagement and emotional attunement that can be built in a close relationship.

This means, no matter what age a person is, it's never too late to use love, affection and human compassion to help shape their brain and psychology. If negative behavioural patterns have developed, such as anxiety, depression, or volatile emotional outburst, they can be aleviated through love and compassionate relationships. As we saw in Chapter 5, the practice of mindfulness also changes the brain neurologically in the same way. The scientific community are now proving what spirituality has taught us since the dawn of time.

For me, this proves what ancient religious texts and religious speakers and teachers have been telling us for hundreds of years, and what I have witnessed from my own work in the field of psychotherapy and mental health: true healing comes from self-awareness, love and compassion.

Time to Connect

So how do you make time for these emotionally attuned family times? Well, once you've learned the art of tuning inwards, connecting to your True Self, then learning to live from a place of groundedness and present-centred awareness, you can apply this state of mind to all activities with your partner and children: bedtime story, bath time, feeding when they're new born, to making time to eat together when they're teens. Times of conflict and discord even become the best times to step into your spiritual growth because it's at these times your connection with your True Self and awareness of your Ego triggers really come into their own.

If you can bring full awareness to your triggers, recognise them and name them, then you can stop your Ego being the parent and can connect to your child from a place that is only love and acceptance. We're all learning and so we all need patience and acceptance, but our children need it the most from us. What better lesson to leave them with: to prioritise this connection, this present-centred grounded time together, to absorb and enjoy the moment with no distractions and no projections of Ego, is so fulfilling and joyous as a mother. Nothing on this earth will fill you with the same level of contentment.

When I had my children, I knew this in every fibre of my body, but I could also feel the pressure of our society pulling me away from them, triggering my Ego. I had to work hard to trust my Inner Teacher and give myself that time to just be with and enjoy my children. I look back now and I still feel that I missed so much. Some of you out there, I know, can't help that you have to work, and, like myself, even need to work for some sense of self, so I'm not saying don't work, don't have hobbies, or don't leave your child's side. That's not my message. What I'm saying is: make the time to be purely and passionately present with them, remember quality versus quantity, and make sure to absorb the love and the special, priceless moments you have together.

Make time for them and learn how to cultivate that ability to let go of all distractions to be present with your children. Not feeling the need to do or instruct in any way.

Simply be. Using everything you've learned in this book, be in the moment, watching, observing, smelling, hearing, noticing. Use all your senses to drink them into your heart and hold that glorious feeling within. That feeling can never be lost, no matter how much time passes. This is the gift of life, this feeling of love and expansion. This is what being a mother is all about. Practise this, and the practicalities of schooling, swimming lessons and all the other 'to do' things on your list just fall into place.

Meditation Exercise

This exercise is an inter-connected meditation exercise to get you started, using your meditation of self-blending into your relationship with your child.

Choose a convenient time, turn off all phones, televisions and any distractions. As a parent, communicate to your child that this is your quality time together and it is a time for you to be completely undistracted. Explain to your child that you're here, you see them, you hear them, you're present. The activity can be anything chosen by the child. This is because we often tell children, and even young adults, what they have to do. They rarely have the opportunity to completely lead the time they spend in parent or adult company, so allow it now. This gives them a sense of control, empowerment and it's a little wink towards trust, appreciation and respect, too.

Once you have chosen your activity, it's important to ground yourself in the present moment so you don't become distracted by your own mind. You do this by taking the time to observe and notice the child, as if you're seeing them for the first time. So, take yourself back to the day they were born and see them as if for the first time. Cultivate that feeling you had when you first held them in your arms, the first time you smelled them and felt their little heart beat close to yours. Take time to notice something about them that you haven't noticed before. This helps you see them with fresh eyes. It also helps you remain grounded in the moment.

Make sure to let them lead the conversation and the time you have together (if it's safe to do so, of course). Listen carefully and thoughtfully, making sure to occasionally reflect back to them what they are saying, and what you're hearing. Be careful not to lead the conversation or questions in any way. Simply listen and be present.

End this time together with a hug that lasts as long as you child would like it to. Saying things such as, 'I love you,' or, 'I appreciate you,' are a beautiful way to connect. These sentiments are often taken for granted but are very powerful and should be used wisely. If you can hold the embrace, see if you can feel the beat of your child's heart, and try to mimic their breathing.

Try to make this time together every day, no matter what. You can get really creative with this exercise and it can be applied to most activities and all ages. As long as you understand the 'letting go of the need to control the activity, the seeing them with fresh eyes, and the noticing and observing them' part, the rest of the exercise is adaptable.

You Are a Spiritual Being Having an Incredible Human Experience

I want to end this book by simply reminding you that you weren't born to live an unhealthy life of misery.

You're a spiritual being having a human experience and your life is literally in your own hands and designed by your own thoughts, which then affect how you feel and the choices you make, moment to moment and every day.

Thoughts of insecurity and fear lead to anger, jealousy, resentment, lack of confidence, and victim mentality. These low vibrational thoughts and feelings cause you to self-sabotage because of your reactive behaviours that come from such toxic and often all-encompassing feelings. This then leads to more negative, fear-based thinking and entrenched beliefs – and the cycle repeats itself. This is a true model of psychology and behavioural patterns; it's the basis of Cognitive Behavioural Therapy.

Understanding this model and following a good psychotherapeutic plan to change these thoughts and affect behavioural change is helpful. But, as you've probably gathered by now, it's not enough.This CBT model has been adapted from spiritual wisdom, but the most important parts were left out. The keys to this model working on all levels are these:

1. Open up your heart.
2. Reconnect to your True Self so that toxic, negative thoughts are revealed to be nothing more than what they are: fear and illusion.

3. Return to God by inviting Divine love into your life.
4. Commit to living a life of truth and authenticity and to serving all beings through achieving your dreams and true purpose.

This is the secret to true happiness, health and total abundance.

It's my life's purpose to help you achieve those and I hope this book has gone a little way towards doing that. If it has then I'll be very happy.

Please remember, never settle for less, never believe you can't, because you always can! And never, ever let anyone else put you down. You were born to heal this world for our children of tomorrow. Your abundance and happiness are your Divine birthright, no matter what 2000 years of manipulation have said and, no matter what crap you see in the media, your True Self knows the truth. You just need to exercise your free will and choose to get out of your own way so you can absolutely and consciously create a life you love! And, yes, even if you have kids – in fact, especially if you have kids.

Bonus Chapter

Essential Oils to Heal and Transform Your Life and Raise Your Spiritual Vibration

Irrespective of the differences in all spiritual practices and teachings, one thing they all have in common that has been practised since human beings began to record their lives, is the use of fragrance and essential oils within the spiritual practice.

I have included this chapter as a bonus. As you've seen, after every practice or exercise, I have suggested various essential oils you can diffuse or blend together for massage to enhance that practice. This chapter is to provide you with a little more information around essential oils and how to use them safely.

For me, essential oils elevate my spiritual and healing practices. I use them when I pray, meditate and ignite the Holy Fire when offering healing to myself and others. Essential oils are very much a part of the practices of The Way of the Rose as it is said the Magdalene was a student of the temple of Isis, where essential oils were used to help others connect to their True Selves, heart centres and the heavens.

Essential oils are very much a part of my life and I'm honoured to share a little about them with you here in this bonus chapter. However, this is only a summary and brief introduction to the wonderous properties of these magical, aromatic compounds, so if this is something that strikes a chord with you and you want to know more about them, I highly recommend you read the work of Valerie Ann Worwood, who is an authority on the subject.

A Brief History of Essential Oils

Historically, essential oils have been used since the dawn of time for medicinal and healing purposes. Today they're gaining in popularity as people come to realise the power of plants! So, as more people wake up and choose a natural-based lifestyle, this is leading to greater health and, ultimately, happiness.

The use of essential oils can be dated back to the 12th century in early Middle Eastern civilisations. However, some research points towards essential oils being used much earlier. I believe essential oils were certainly used during the time of Mary Magdalene and before. As a follower of the Divine feminine and The Way Of The Rose I use essential oils to elevate my consciousness and connect with the Divine when meditating and channelling the Magdalene. Since I've been doing this, I've experienced deep shifts in my awareness and connection to Divine love and my True Self. I also use them with clients, many of whom have experienced their benefits with mental, emotional and physical health issues.

We know ancient Egyptians used essential oils as they believed the sense of smell was the most important and most powerful of all the senses. The High Priestesses of Isis used oils as part of their rituals and practices calling on the Divine feminine. Mary Magdalene is believed to have been trained in these ancient mystical traditions, using oils for healing by helping others connect to their True Selves and Divine love, as well as helping the dying transcend to the next life.

The Bible clearly states Mary Magdalene used Spikenard to bathe Jesus Christ's body following the crucifixion. Some believe this was to follow the Soul midwifery tradition in helping him move on to the spiritual world; however, others believe essential oils were used for their healing properties to help him rise, along with life force energy healing, which today would be known as Reiki.

I know what I believe. As a dedicated follower of The Way of the Rose, and someone who channels the Magdalene, essential oils are essential to my way of life and my work.

Throughout this book I have included various essential oil recipes to help you go deeper in your journey. For me, essential oils are a daily component within my practice that elevate me to a higher spiritual level than I thought possible. They are great for supporting better, more balanced emotional health and this is again proven as we know essential oils change the chemistry of the brain through the olfactory bulb in the nose. They also stimulate and enhance your consciousness on a vibrational level.

When learning about essential oils it's important to

understand a little history about where they come from and how we use them today. To understand the full and amazing health benefits of integrating essential oils into your life and home, you should know about their physical properties and what they are. Not many people (believe it or not) realise essential oils originally come from plants and flowers.

Essential oils are highly concentrated oils extracted from plants and flowers, and are considered to be the 'essence' of the plant from which they have been extracted; therefore, they are extremely potent. They are highly beneficial for you physically, mentally and spiritually.

You only need to use a very small amount to receive huge benefits to your overall health and well-being.

Essential Oils Today

Although the practice of aromatherapy dates back to ancient times, it was not until the 20th century that modern scientists began to support the idea of using essential oils for health benefits. In the early 1990s, substantial research helped biologists better understand how the brain reacts to aromas.

This research proved what people of ancient civilisations had already put into practice – essential oils can be used to create positive healing responses within the body. Today, there is a lot of research and investigation concerning essential oils with researchers being continually surprised by the results.

For example, Frankincense (known as the king of oils) is proven to have a dramatic effect on strengthening your immune system and cellular functioning. Because of this ongoing research the field of essential oils is greatly expanding.

The Benefits of Essential Oils

The regular use of essential oils can have lasting benefits and can be used for many different purposes.

For example, they can benefit mental health, physical health, increase energy and propel your connection to your True Self and the Divine to a higher level.

For example, I often get clients struggling with meditation because their mind is so highly agitated it's a struggle to sit and try to focus.

Essential oils can provide a calming, grounding platform, helping you untangle yourself from your racing mind and the often-paralysing effects of anxiety and chronic stress. This then allows you to start the practice of focussing your mind and meditating.

Alternatively, another example is if you want to feel energised, motivated and inspired, there are essential oils to help you cultivate this mood and energy, too.

You can also use essential oils for soothing cuts, infections, coughs, colds and viruses, improving health and vitality through regular use and, of course, good nutrition. You can even introduce them into your beauty care and home cleaning products to reduce the toxic load in your environment and your home and replace it with plant-based compounds.

They really are incredible on so many levels; this little bonus chapter couldn't possibly do them full justice in helping you understand their full capacity and benefits. At the end of the chapter I'll leave a list for further resources that I love.

Not all Oils are Equal

At this point I think it's a great time to mention that not all oils are equal. You may buy oils you believe are essential oils and are going to help detox and improve your health, but it's so important to understand that not all oils are essential oils. Some oils are purely fragrance oils and have synthetics in them which make them artificial and really not good for you to inhale and certainly not to ingest.

These oils have no plant power at all. They're usually opted for because they're super cheap, but really it makes no sense because 1) you're not getting real essential oils, so you're not getting the healing benefits of plant power that you may be looking for; and 2) good quality essential oils are incredibly potent, so you only ever need to use a tiny amount to achieve your desired results and benefits.

The essential oils I use and recommend are not only organic, they're of a certified therapeutic grade; this means they're better than organic.

They're the highest standard of oils that are produced. For me, there are no other oils that I would use on my family or myself.

Whatever essential oils you choose to use, my advice is to stay away from anything synthetic... you just don't know what you're inhaling, and you certainly shouldn't use them for anything else. Always go organic and above.

The Three Ways

There are three ways you can typically use essential oils. These are:

Aromatically: as in aromatherapy, where you inhale the oil for its benefits.

Topically: where you can use the oil on your body in some way, usually with a carrier oil.

Internally: where you ingest the oils. Obviously, take care to check each individual oil to ensure this is safe.

Aromatically

There are a few different methods of diffusing essential oils around the home. You can use a diffuser, or put some oil onto cotton wool balls and place them around a room (take care not to use on wooden surfaces).

Topically

Add a few drops to a base blending oil (carrier oil), such as Sweet Almond oil or Jojoba oil, and apply to:

Neck.

Forehead and temples.

Chest and abdomen.

Arms, legs, bottom of feet.

Not all essential oils should be applied directly to your skin. Most oils are very potent and need to be diluted with a base blending oil, as above, before being massaged into skin. Always read the instructions and, if in doubt, ask advice.

When adding to bath water, use sparingly – a few drops are usually enough – and always use a dispersant. Essential oils do not dissolve in water. They sit on the top of it, and so if you put some into your bath water – think about what part of your body goes in first, and then second. If you're like me, once your feet are in, you sit down. So, undiluted oil will go straight onto your bottom, and will be heated (unless you're in a cold bath). This can cause irritation. So, be safe: put a few drops into a dispersant first and *then* put that in the bath. The Tisserand Institute – www.tisserand.com – has recipes and advice. And Robert Tisserand's blog – www.roberttisserand.com – is full of interesting information. Did you know sniffing Rosemary essential oil can enhance your memory by 75%?

Be Sure to Avoid: some facial areas, such as the skin around the eyes.
Eyes and inner ears.
Broken, damaged, or otherwise injured skin.

How to use Essential Oils Safely

I've mentioned a lot that quality essential oils are potent, so it's easy to underestimate just how strong they can be. Because of this it's super important to be aware and know that even though the majority of oils are completely safe to use aromatically, and topically – some oils do come with specific warnings, such as photosensitivity on the skin or skin irritation

For this reason, just a reminder, when using aromatherapy oil topically it's important to know when to break it down with a carrier oil. To be safe, the general warning is not to use any oil on your skin that hasn't been diluted with a carrier oil. If you do notice any sensitivity occurring, dilute the oil a little more or stop using it altogether. People with known sensitive skin and allergies should exercise additional caution.

Again, with all essential oils, make sure you avoid contact with your eyes. If you're using them on your face, ensure to dilute them and be extra careful around your whole eye area.

Finally, remember that essential oils are extremely flammable, so always use with caution. Keep them away from direct sunlight.

Also, if you're pregnant, always consult your medical practitioner before using them. The use of essential oils in pregnancy is very much under debate by those who know more than I. Some use, and swear by them, and some don't; always discuss with your doctor or midwife and do your research before making your decision.

Where to Start: The Most Common Essential Oils

Now we've looked at the benefits of using essential oils and ways in which to use them and, of course, using them safely, let's look at the most common essential oils, and those I recommend you start with.

Bergamot: an essential oil which originates in citrus trees, with a scent that enhances your sense of peace and happiness. I use Bergamot a lot when I meditate as it helps me tune inwards and connect to my True Self. For this reason, it's excellent to improve low mood and depression. It's also a fabulous antiseptic.

Clove: Clove essential oil is a fabulous antioxidant and has pain-relieving properties. Ever been to the dentist and had clove put into a filling? When you use it in your diffuser it helps kill airborne microorganisms... great to use when the norovirus is present in your home to help prevent it from spreading like a bush fire! It's also a great mouth cleanser too, just add a drop to your toothpaste, or add a drop to water to swill around your mouth after brush. For safety reasons, swill for a few minutes then spit out.

Eucalyptus: one of the most common essential oils and used in almost every household even if you don't realise it. It's a powerful oil for respiratory issues, coughs, colds, and scratchy, itchy sore throats etc Gargle, spit out and don't swallow.

Frankincense: the Don of all essential oils, Frankincense is fabulous for the immune system, for your skin and for deepening your spiritual awareness and improving your mental and emotional health. This is a particular favourite of mine.

Lavender: the most commonly used essential oil and the one I remember growing up with in my home. My mum seemed to smell of lavender all the time. It's used for balance and peace, which is why it's a great aide for settling the children at night and getting some sleep yourself. This oil can also help with spiritual growth, letting go of unwanted negative emotions, treat insect bites and even treat dandruff.

Lemon: repels insects naturally and is a fabulous natural home cleaner!

Oregano: is fabulous for immunity, muscle tension, opening up the respiratory system to help you breathe and helps you cultivate a sense of safety and security. **Top Tip**: put on the bottom of your feet when you first feel the chills or scratchy throat of an emerging virus in your body.

Peppermint: great for an upset tummy, indigestion, nausea, cramping, headaches – Peppermint tackles them all. It contains lots of nutrients such as vitamin C and potassium and is one of the oldest essential oils used today. It's abundant as it's one of the easiest oils to extract from leaves and bark, which also makes it one of the cheapest to source.

Rosemary: is a great oil for improving mood, positivity and energy. A lovely one to aromatically dress yourself with in the mornings after a shower. And, as I mentioned earlier, repeated research shows it is also beneficial for memory.

Tea Tree (Melaleuca): Tea Tree always brings back beautiful memories of Australia for me, where this plant originates. It's a microbial, which is great for skin conditions. This is one essential oil that you must NEVER ingest as it can be toxic.

Buying and Storing Essential Oils

Buying

Make sure you know where you're getting your oils from and make sure they're of the highest quality that you can afford.

Remember cheaper is NEVER better with essential oils. You want to go for quality over quantity every time for optimal health and well-being effects.

Storing

Finally, when mixing your essential oils only store them in dark glass or stainless-steel bottles, otherwise the oils will react to the packaging. Keep them out of direct sunlight and heat.

Summary

I hope this has been a helpful introduction to the power of plants and the health benefits of essential oils. Once you start on your journey, I guarantee you'll fall in love with the plant power of essential oils and become a bonafide essential oils junkie like me. It really is a truly beautiful way of life.

If you've enjoyed what you've read, understand the amazing benefits that integrating essential oils into your home and family life can have, and would like more information about how I can help you get started on your essential oil journey with the certified therapeutic grade essential oils, visit my website aimeeleighsmith.com.

Further Reading

I have loved every minute of writing this book. Well, almost. Every minute between the tears and tantrums anyway. It's my greatest hope that you have found it helpful in getting out of your own way to live a life you love, a life you absolutely deserve and which is your Divine right.

I've referred to a few books and authors who have inspired me on my journey and, as promised, here are my suggestions for your own further reading. Some of these are extremely famous and you've probably heard of them; others not so much, but still extremely valuable in opening your eyes to a deeper universal wisdom.

In no particular order

A Return to Love by Marianne Williamson. In my opinion an absolute must for anyone who wants to understand themselves better and live a happier life.

The Power of Now by Eckhart Tolle. Again, another very famous and truly fabulous book. In my opinion this book helps you understand the idea of living in the present moment better than most because it cuts out a lot of fluff and jargon.

Awakening the Buddha Within: Tibetan Wisdom for the Western World by Lama Surya Das. This book is still a check-in book for me today. Any time I need a good reminder I turn to the beautiful and easy-to-understand teachings of the Buddha. Lama Surya Das has a way of simplifying often quite complex belief systems and helps you understand their relevance to modern living. Whenever I read anything of his I always feel at peace.

Buddha's Brain by Rick Hanson, PhD. This is a great book that helps you understand the neurological effects of mindfulness. It's brain science made simple.

Wherever You Go, There You Are: Mindfulness Meditation in Everyday Life by Jon Kabat-Zinn.

The Ecstasy of Surrender by Judith Orloff M.D. A very relatable and easy-to-understand book on how surrender can affect our whole lives and pave the way for emotional freedom.

Self-Compassion: The Proven Power of Being Kind to Yourself by Dr Kristin Neff.

The Conscious Parent: Transforming Ourselves, Empowering Our Children by Dr Shefali Tsabary, PhD. A book every parent should read. You all had a mum and dad and their parenting has affected you. This book explains how you project that effect on to your children. Dr Shefali has lots of really awesome videos on YouTube, too.

Dark Nights of the Soul by Thomas Moore. This book is a spiritual staple in understanding that the difficult times in our lives are just as important, valid and in some ways as beautiful as the good times. An absolute must read!

Women Who Run with the Wolves by Clarissa Pinkola Estés, PhD. I first read this as a young woman and it blew my mind. It still does today. It's another book I often refer back to and find deeper meaning in the moment I need it. Every woman should read this, especially our young women.

The Meaning of Mary Magdalene by Cynthia Bourgeault. What can I say, this book shook my world, and it validates my whole spiritual purpose and work. It's not 'out there', like some other Magdalene books, the author is a scholar and well respected. She gives historically accurate information and delivers some controversial and often hard-to-understand connections, easily making it simpler for the readers' light bulbs to switch on and for them to see the truth. If you want to learn the truth about 'the way' from a truly trusted source, this is the book for you.

The Secret Teachings of Mary Magdalene by Claire Nahmad & Margaret Bailey. I love this book but it *is* a little out there. If you're into that then you'll love its insights.

The Magdalen Manuscript: *The Alchemies of Horus & The Sex Magic of Isis* by Tom Kenyon and Judi Sion. Another great book about the Magdalene and Jesus. This is specifically about their Tantric relationship and the truth of their teachings. Again, this book is a little out there, so not for the faint-hearted, but I loved it.

Labyrinth: Your Path to Self Discovery by Tony Christie.

The Fragrant Mind and *The Fragrant Heavens* by Valerie Ann Worwood. These two amazing books talk about how essential oils support your emotional health and spiritual growth.

About the Author

Aimee Leigh is a mental health nurse, psychotherapist, yoga teacher and Reiki Holy Fire Master. Aimee Leigh has worked in mental health services and private practice for eighteen years.

Printed in Great
Britain
by Amazon

31856397R00147